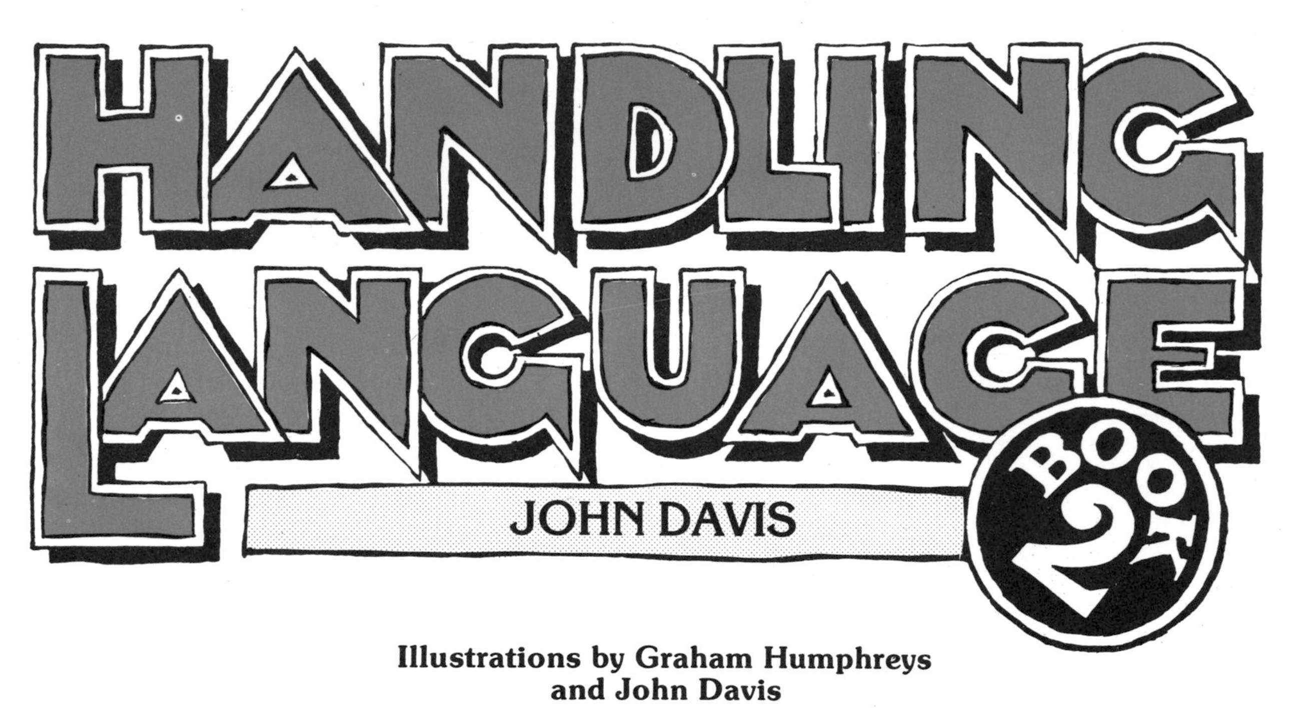

Illustrations by Graham Humphreys
and John Davis

Stanley Thornes (Publishers) Ltd

Originally published in 1982 by Hutchinson Education
Reprinted 1983, 1984, 1986

Reprinted in 1990 by
Stanley Thornes (Publishers) Ltd
Old Station Drive
Leckhampton
CHELTENHAM GL53 0DN

British Library Cataloguing in Publication Data

Davis, John
Handling Language
2
1. English language—Grammar—1950—
I. Title
428.2 PE1112

ISBN 0 7487 0239 3

Printed and bound in Great Britain at
Martin's of Berwick

*To my grandsons
Daniel Benjamin and
Michael Alexander*

Also by the same author:
Handling Language 1
Handling Spelling
Handling Punctuation

CONTENTS

Sentence construction

Special terms

THE HYPHEN

The hyphen makes a compound word from two or more connected words.

1 The hyphen is used to make a compound noun from two connected words, for example:

A *table* for *coffee* is a *coffee-table.*
Someone who *lifts weights* is called a *weight-lifter.*

(a) Write out the following, putting in hyphens where they are required in compound nouns.

1 Teacher: 'Give me the names of three collective nouns.'
Pupil: 'Fly paper, dust bin and vacuum cleaner. They're all "collective".'

2 A glow worm met his friend in the car park. 'You must have been drunk last night,' he said. 'You tried to make friends with a cigarette end.'

2 The hyphen is also used to make a compound adjective from two connected words, for example:

'This bottle is *half-empty!*'
'No it's not. It's *half-full.*'

(b) Write out the following, putting in hyphens where they are required in compound adjectives.

1 What I want for Christmas is a gift wrapped five pound box of money.
2 'I began life as a poor bare footed lad.'
'Well, nobody is born with shoes.'
3 People and stained glass windows should be judged in their best light.
4 Sign on a street market stall: 'Feather filled quilts. Buy before the prices rise and down goes up.'

(c) Put the following compound adjectives into sentences of your own.

half-hearted	thick-skinned
slow-witted	high-handed
south-west	reddish-brown
burning-hot	icy-cold

(d) Sometimes groups of three of four words are joined with hyphens to make longer compound adjectives. Write out the following, joining the groups with hyphens.

1 She was a happy go lucky girl.
2 I will see you in the not too distant future.
3 He left home and became a good for nothing layabout.
4 A do it yourself person hits the nail right on the thumb.
5 Wife to husband: 'You know the new bumper on the car that withstands a five mile an hour impact? Well, the garage door doesn't.'

3 The hyphen is used in writing fractions, for example: *three-quarters*, and in writing compound numbers, for example: *ninety-nine.*

(e) Write out the following, putting in hyphens where they are required.

1 'Didn't I tell you to notice when the soup boiled over?'
'I did, Mum. It was ten thirty.'
2 He didn't know four sixths was the same as two thirds until his dad bought him a pocket calculator.
3 When he was twenty one he was a seven stone weakling; now, at the age of forty five, he's a fourteen stone weakling.

4 The hyphen is used to attach a prefix to a word in order to alter the meaning.

re **+** *entered* **= re-entered**
co **+** *operate* **= co-operate**
pre **+** *school* **= pre-school**
ex **+** *captain* **= ex-captain**

The hyphen is used to prevent any ambiguity.

(f) Write out the following, filling in the blank spaces with appropriate words from the list below. For example:

resigned re-signed

'All the Arsenal players have *resigned.* I'm sorry, I'll read that again. All the Arsenal players have *re-signed.*'

striking-clock	cross section
recover	man-eating
cross-section	striking clock
man eating	re-cover

1 The hire-purchase company sent two of their men to ——— the furniture. The upholstery repairers sent two of their men to ——— the furniture.
2 How magnificent that ——— would look on my mantelpiece; I wonder if it is actually a ———.
3 If you take a ——— of people who have been waiting for hours for a delayed train, you will find that they are indeed a very ——— of people.
4 At the zoo, this morning, I saw a ——— fish in the aquarium; this afternoon, in the restaurant, I saw a ——— fish.

(g) For revision practice, write out the following, putting in hyphens where they are required.

1 He's so lazy, it takes him five minutes to boil a three minute egg.
2 'I say, can you lend me £10 for a month, old boy?'
'What does a month old boy want with £10?'
3 Notice in the window of a second hand shop: 'Mrs Smith has cast off clothing of every description.'

A syllable is a unit of pronunciation; for example, the word *banana* consists of three syllables: *ba-na-na.*

1 You will be aware of the number of syllables in words from the 'metre' of poetry. In lines like:

The curfew tolls the knell of parting day,
The lowing herd winds slowly o'er the lea,
The ploughman homeward plods his weary way,
And leaves the world to darkness and to me.

there are the same number of syllables in each line. This gives the poetry its rhythm.

2 A dictionary shows you how words are divided into syllables. In order to show you how to pronounce a word, the dictionary puts a stress mark after the main syllable, for example: chil′blain cabb′age syll′able

3 You also have to think about syllables when you don't have enough space for a long word on the end of a line, and you have to split it with a hyphen.

The following five points will help you decide where to place the hyphen:

1 Never divide words of only one syllable, such as *eighth, height.*

2 Do not divide endings which are not sounded as a separate syllable, such as burn-ed.

3 Do not divide proper names.

4 Never divide a word so that a single letter ends one line or begins the next, such as a-round , read-y

5 Try to divide words (if really necessary) so that *both parts may be pronounced.* The hyphen should come between separate syllables, and when you are in doubt, consult your dictionary.

COMPOUND WORDS

Not all compound words are still linked by hyphens; some are now so familiar that they are run together as one word. You can always check the punctuation in a dictionary.

'What is your profession?'
'I'm editor of a newspaper.*'*
'Is that so? Well I am a chief, and soon you will be editor-in-chief!*'*

(a) Write out the following, deciding whether the compound words need hyphens.

1 He is *knockkneed, crosseyed, overweight* and *bigheaded* – and those are his good points.
2 There are three kinds of people: *righthanded, lefthanded* and *underhanded.*
3 Did you hear about the man who had an *eighteencarat, dustproof, shockproof, waterproof, nonwinding, antimagnetic* watch? He lost it!
4 *twentyfive, broadminded, rearview, vicepresident, spaceship, countdown, supermarket, cloakroom, thirdclass.*

(b) Write out the following, putting the *compound words* listed below in the blank spaces.

lion-tamer	toothpaste	fourth-form
bookworm	half-sisters	wishbone
night-club	tee-shirt	dishwater
knot-holes	cigarette-lighter	

1 'Daddy, what are those holes for in this plank of wood?'
'Those are ——— .'
'Well, if they are *not holes,* what are they?'
2 'Your husband reads a great deal. Is he a ——— ?'
'No, just an ordinary one.'
3 'Waiter! This soup tastes like ——— .'
'Really, sir? And how do you know?'
4 'Do you stock a Superman ——— in a small size?
5 'That chicken I bought had no ——— !'
'Sorry, madam. Perhaps it no longer had anything to wish for.'
6 'How do you make a ——— ?'
'Easy: take out the tobacco.'
7 Mr Smith has become a ——— . He used to teach the ——— but lost his nerve and gave up teaching.
8 'What pearly teeth you have, little girl! Do you use ——— ?'
'What for? My teeth aren't loose.'
9 'I am a ——— magician; I saw a woman in half.'
'Where did you learn the trick?'
'At home, where I still live with my four ——— ,'

1 To form the *plural* of a compound word, care must be taken to add the plural 's' to the correct part of the word, for example, 'brother-in-law, becomes 'brothers-in-law'. (You mean more than one *brother,* not more than one law.)

For compound words without hyphens, simply add 's' to form the plural, for example, 'stepdaughter' becomes 'stepdaughters'. (You mean more than one *daughter,* not more than one step.)

'Spoonful' becomes 'spoonfuls'. (You mean there is not more than one spoon.)

The dash is used to indicate a sudden break in thought. It is useful in introducing the unexpected but it *must* be used *very sparingly.*

1 . An example of the dash used to indicate a *break in the sequence of the sentence*:

There are three things I always forget: names, faces, and – the third I can't remember.

(a) The following include breaks in sequence. Write them out, putting in the dash where appropriate.

1. Keep smiling it makes people wonder what you have been up to.
2. A melon for a penny and if you haven't a penny?
3. It takes two to speak the truth one to speak and one to hear.
4. Visits always give pleasure if not the arrival, then the departure.
5. We all remain better friends at a slight distance.
6. It is not true that a lazy pupil never thinks; he is always thinking about something else.
7. Living in the past has one advantage in its favour it's cheaper.
8. The world gets better every day then worse again in the evening.
9. I can sum the situation up in one word indescribable!
10. And lo! I heard a voice inside me say, 'Smile! Things could be worse.' So I smiled and they got worse.

2 Examples of the dash used to introduce *the unexpected*:

He loves her for what she is – rich.

The trouble with him is he bites off more than he can chew – and then chews it.

(b) Write out the following, putting in the dash where appropriate.

1. My uncle died of a sore throat my auntie cut it.
2. I can't understand why most people won't admit their faults because I would if I had any.
3. 'Don't come down the ladder, I've taken it away.'
   'Too late I'm halfway down.'
4. 'Do any of your relatives come to see you in prison?
   'They don't have to they're all here.'
5. 'Daddy, there's a black cat in the dining-room.'
   'Never mind, black cats are lucky.'
   'This one is he's eaten your dinner.'
6. 'All our greatest men are dead! Drake, Nelson, Wellington I'm not feeling too well myself.'
7. Some teachers have terrible memories they never forget anything.

(c) Write out the following, putting in two dashes where appropriate.

1. Judge: 'I'm amazed how could you possibly acquit the accused?'
   Jury Foreman: 'Insanity, your Honour.'
   Judge: 'What all of you?'
2. 'I'm going to the doctor I don't like the look of my husband.'
   'I'll come with you I hate the sight of mine.'

A parenthesis is an explanation or a piece of extra information included within a sentence. It is separated from the main sentence by being put between (a) a pair of commas, (b) a pair of dashes, or (c) a pair of brackets.

Note: If you take away the words in parenthesis, the rest of the sentence should still make complete sense.

1 The pair of commas is used when the separated material is fairly close to the main meaning of the sentence. For example:

Gossip, *unlike river water*, flows both ways.

(a) Write out the following, putting in the commas to indicate parenthesis.

1. He decided having carefully considered the situation to postpone the event until next week.
2. The law in its majestic equality forbids the rich as well as the poor to sleep under the arches.
3. Population when unchecked increases in a geometrical ratio. Subsistence on the other hand only increases in an arithmetical ratio.

2 The pair of dashes is used to put an after-thought, an interruption or an explanation into a sentence. For example:

What are know as citrus fruits – *oranges, lemons, grapefruits* – are very rich in vitamin C.

(b) Write out the following, putting in the dashes to indicate parenthesis.

1. He says I hope he is right that these samples are free.
2. It's a very odd thing as odd as can be that whatever Miss T. eats turns into Miss T.

3 The pair of brackets is the strongest form of parenthesis. This form should be reserved only for cases where there is a definite intrusion (often including a verb) into the thought of the sentence. For example:

I took 50p (*all I had in my pocket*) and handed it to the flag-seller.

(c) Write out the following, putting in the brackets to indicate parenthesis.

1. He searched the desks all the cupboards were locked and found the missing books.
2. Smith and Jones Jones scored two goals both played a good game.
3. Fill in the coupon in ink pencil will not do and send it to the pools-promoters.

The pair of brackets are also used in drama-writing, to separate stage directions. For example:

Teacher *(rapping on desk)*:'Come on, now! Order, please!'
Voice *(from the back of the class)*: 'I'll take a hamburger with chips.'

4. Customer: 'What flavours of ice-cream have you today?'
   Pretty young waitress speaking in a hoarse whisper: 'Vanilla, chocolate and strawberry.'
   Customer in a sympathetic tone of voice: 'Have you got laryngitis?'
   Waitress: 'Just vanilla, chocolate and strawberry.'

The semi-colon joins together clauses which are closely related and are of equal weight.

1 Examples:

Entrances are wide; exits are narrow.

Man eats to live; he does not live to eat.

If you have wisdom, what do you lack;
if you lack wisdom, what do you have?

Note: Both clauses must be able to stand as separate sentences. The semi-colon is chosen when a full stop would be too strong a break and a comma would be too weak.

(a) Write out the following, putting in the semi-colon where required.

1 Marriage is a very fine institution no family should be without one.
2 Opportunity only knocks temptation kicks down the door.
3 I love television close your eyes and it's almost as good as radio.
4 No man is the whole of himself his friends are the rest of him.
5 If you are idle, be not solitary if you are solitary, be not idle.
6 When you laugh, everyone sees when you weep, no one notices.
7 Love looks through a telescope envy looks through a microscope.
8 To love is to admire with the heart to admire is to love with the mind.
9 Life can only be understood backwards it must be lived forwards.
10 When befriended, remember it when you befriend, forget it.
11 In peace, sons bury their fathers in war, fathers bury their sons.
12 In youth, one has tears without grief in age, grief without tears.
13 To be born a gentleman is an accident to die one, an achievement.
14 Deep doubts, deep wisdom small doubts, little wisdom.
15 A wise man knows everything a shrewd man knows everybody.
16 Wise men talk because they have something to say fools, because they have to say something.
17 Wise men learn by other men's mistakes fools learn by their own.
18 The luck of having talent is not enough one must also have a talent for luck.
19 Never trust a man who speaks well of everybody he who praises everybody praises nobody.
20 Talent without genius isn't much genius without talent is nothing.
21 Exercise is unnecessary. If you are healthy you don't need it if you are ill, you shouldn't take it.
22 Streams become crooked from taking the path of least resistance it is the same with people.

(b) Write out some sentences of your own, using a semi-colon to join up two clauses which are closely related and of equal weight.

2 More than one semi-colon may be used if there is a sequence of clauses of equal weight.

Examples:

I wish I loved the Human Race;
I wish I loved its silly face;
I wish I liked the way it walks;
I wish I liked the way it talks;
And when I'm introduced to one
I wish I thought 'What Jolly Fun'!

Laugh and the world laughs with you;
Weep, and you weep alone;
For the sad old earth must borrow its mirth,
But has trouble enough of its own.

Youth is a blunder; manhood is a struggle; old age a regret.

(c) Write out the following, putting in semi-colons where required.

1 For want of a nail the shoe was lost for want of a shoe the horse was lost for want of a horse the rider was lost and for want of a rider the battle was lost.
2 The old believe everything the middle-aged suspect everything the young know everything.
3 Children begin by loving their parents after a time they judge them rarely, if ever, do they forgive them.
4 The lights begin to twinkle from the rocks the long day wanes the slow moon climbs some stars faintly appear the deep moans round with many voices.
5 It is not good for all your wishes to be fulfilled: through sickness you recognise the value of health through evil, the value of good through exertion, the value of rest.
6 Youth is not enough love is not enough and, if possible, enough would not be enough.

(d) Write out some sentences of your own, using semi-colons as shown.

3 Semi-colons are also used to separate long items in a list.

First here is an example of a list where commas alone do not make the sense completely clear:

For your art-work you will need: a white canvas on a stretcher, some sticks of charcoal, three sizes of brushes, preferably hog-hair, oil-paints in the primary colours, plus black and white, a little linseed-oil and turpentine, and a great deal of imagination.

Here is the same piece, using semi-colons to make the separate items clearer:

For your art-work you will need: a white canvas on a stretcher; some sticks of charcoal; three sizes of brushes, preferably hog-hair; oil-paints in the primary colours, plus black and white; a little linseed-oil and turpentine; and a great deal of imagination.

(e) Write out the following, replacing commas with semi-colons where necessary to make the sense clear.

1 The advantages of a bad memory are: one cannot be a good liar, one cannot tell long boring stories, one forgets offences, and one enjoys places and books a second time round.
2 A group of cinema engineers classified the following as the ten most dramatic sounds in films: a baby's first cry, the blast of a siren, the galloping of horses, the howl of a dog, the sound of a distant train whistle, the thunder of breakers on rocks, the roar of a forest fire, the boom of a ship's fog-horn, the slow drip of water, and, most dramatic of all, the wedding march.
3 There's a new alarm-clock which rings five minutes before getting-up time, right on getting-up time, again, five minutes after getting-up time. You had better switch it off then, if you don't, it phones your school and makes an excuse for your being late.

THE COLON

The colon takes you forward!

The colon carries the first part of a sentence forward to the details or information following.

1 The colon is often used in the form of an 'introduction'.

Introducing speech:
Teacher to pupils, on entering:
'Good morning, boys and girls.'

Introducing an explanation:
'Why Husbands Get into Debt:
Journalist's Wife on Hire-Purchase.'

Introducing quotations:

At Gettysburg, in 1863, Abraham Lincoln said:
'Fourscore and seven years ago our fathers brought forth upon this continent a new nation...'

Introducing a list of items:
Work spares us from the three great evils: boredom, vice and need.

For sale: unused dumb-bells, weights, hand-grips and chest-expander. Owner unable to get lid off box.

(a) Write out the following, using the colon to introduce a list or an explanation.

1 There are two classes of people in the world those who divide the people of the world into two classes and those who do not.
2 The two occasions when a man should not gamble when he can't afford it and when he can.
3 There are three ways to get a job done do it yourself, employ someone else, or tell your children that they must not do it.

2 The colon is also used to link two clauses where the first is dependent on the second for its explanation. The colon leads you forward to the second clause.

For example

Take care of the minutes: *hours will take care of themselves.*

The doorman threw my coat out of the door: *I happened to be in it at the time.*

(b) Write out the following, using the colon where required.

1 The world is a collection of cogs each depends on the other.
2 Some people are like new shoes the cheaper they are the louder they squeak.
3 Worry is like a rocking-chair it gives you something to do, but it won't get you anywhere.
4 Look at me I worked my way up from nothing to a state of poverty.
5 We fear something before we hate it the child who fears noises becomes an adult who hates noise.
6 Do not threaten a child either punish him or forgive him
7 Don't tell your friends their social faults they will cure the fault and never forgive you.
8 All passions exaggerate it is because they do that they are passions.
9 The biggest foolishness of the fool is this he thinks he's smart.
10 There is one great mistake you can make in life continually fearing you will make a mistake.

(c) Write a few sentences of your own using colons in different ways.

3 There are times when you may not be sure whether to use a colon or a semi-colon.

The *colon* is like a spring-board: you land on it and are propelled forward; the *semi-colon* is like the pivot of a sea-saw: it enables two sides to balance each other. You must decide whether the phrases are equally balanced (semi-colon) or have one phrase leading on to another (colon).

Here is an example of both:
One must not become attached to animals: they do not last long enough; or to people: they last too long.

(d) Write out the following, using colons or semi-colons where required.

1 'That's a fine dog you have there it's a bulldog, isn't it?'
'It's not a bulldog it was chasing a cat and ran into a brick wall.'
2 Two men look out through the same bars one sees the mud one sees the stars.
3 Only one type of worry is correct to worry because you worry too much.
4 Ambition is like a treadmill it knows no limits you no sooner get to the end than you begin again.
5 Illness is the most heeded of doctors to wisdom we only make promises pain we obey.
6 The three rudenesses of this world youth mocking at age, health mocking at sickness, a clever man mocking at a poor fool.
7 The three signs of a rogue interrupting during a story, cheating at games, telling offensive jokes.
8 Nothing is truer in a sense than a funeral speech it tells precisely what the dead person should have been.
9 Life is like the Olympic Games a few devote their lives to win a prize the masses just come to watch the show unfold before them.

A row of three dots is technically called an 'ellipsis'. It is used in different ways to indicate *words left out*.

1 The dots are used in dialogue to indicate an interruption. For example:

'Did you see the accused take a gun out of his pocket and...'
'Objection! Defence Counsel is trying to lead the witness.'

'Don't be cowards!' yelled the General. 'Stand up and fight like men! The enemy couldn't hit an elephant at this dist...'

2 The dots are used to indicate that some quoted material has been omitted, or is incomplete. For example:

'If I should die, think only this of me... In hearts at peace, under an English heaven.'

'Friends, Romans, countrymen, lend me your ears...'

3 The dots are used to provide a pause or a special effect. For example:

Tenderfoot in a tough saloon-bar:
'Lemonade...in a dirty glass!'

'Have you had this complaint before?'
'Yes, doctor, about two years ago.'
'Well...er...um...I think you've got it again.'

Somebody's boring me...I think it's me.

4 The dots are used to introduce a surprise ending. For example:

Strip the false tinsel off Hollywood...there's real tinsel underneath.

THE COMMA

First Cat: 'What do commas do?'
Second Cat: 'They give us "pause".'

Some special functions of the comma, such as separating the different items in a list or the different parts of an address on an envelope, or marking off a name or description within a sentence, have been fully dealt with in Book 1.

The comma used as parenthesis is to be found in this book on page 5 and its use in punctuating conversation is to be found on pages 16 and 17.

The comma separates a word, or a group of words, in a sentence, in order to make the meaning clear.

For example:

All generalizations are dangerous, even this one.

He had the sort of face that, once seen, is never remembered.

(a) For revision, write out the sentences on these pages, adding commas where they will make the sense clearer.

To check your answers, you will find that the first five sentences should each have three commas.

1 If one tells the truth one is sure sooner or later to be found out.

2 When you have eliminated the impossible whatever remains however improbable must be the truth.

3 Life is a dream for the wise a game for the fool a comedy for the rich a tragedy for the poor.

4 Is it fair that when a king rules his wife is the queen but when a queen rules her husband is a prince?

5 This time it vanished quite slowly beginning with the end of the tail and ending with the grin which remained some time after the rest of it had gone.

You will find the following sentences need four commas each.

6 At five your son is your master at ten your slave at fifteen your double: after that he is your friend or your enemy depending on how he was raised.

7 Youth which is forgiven everything forgives itself nothing; age which forgives itself everything is forgiven nothing.

8 Of five things have a care: to whom you speak of whom you speak and how and when and where.

9 It is necessary for technical reasons that these boxes should be stored upside down that is with the top at the bottom and the bottom at the top and in order that there may be no doubt as to which is the bottom and which the top for storage purposes it will be seen that the bottom of each box has been labelled with the word 'TOP'.

Write out the following speech made by Sir Winston Churchill in 1940 and put in the eight missing commas.

10 We shall fight in France we shall fight on the seas and oceans we shall fight with growing confidence and growing strength in the air we shall defend our island whatever the cost may be we shall fight on the beaches we shall fight on the landing grounds we shall fight in the fields and in the streets we shall fight in the hills; we shall never surrender.

THE COMMA

Write out the following three verses, putting in the commas that are required.

11 In a cavern by a canyon excavating for a mine
Dwelt a miner Forty-niner and his daughter Clementine.
Oh my darling oh my darling oh my darling Clementine!
Thou art lost and gone for ever!
Dreadful sorry Clementine.

12 Sweet and low sweet and low
Wind of the western sea
Low low breathe and blow
Wind of the the western sea!
Over the rolling waters go
Come from the dying moon and blow
Blow him again to me.

13 Jenny kissed me when we met
Jumping from the chair she sat in;
Time you thief who love to get
Sweets into your list put that in;
Say I'm weary say I'm sad
Say that health and wealth have missed me
Say I'm growing old but add
Jenny kissed me.

Write out the letter that Dr Johnson wrote to Lord Chesterfield in 1755 and put in the ten missing commas.

14 Is not a Patron my Lord one who looks with unconcern on a man struggling for life in the water and when he has reached ground encumbers him with help?

The notice which you have been pleased to take of my labours had it been early had been kind; but it has been delayed till I am indifferent and cannot enjoy it; till I am solitary and cannot impart it; till I am known and do not want it.

(b) Write out a few sentences of your own, using commas where they are needed. Try to say *why* each is there, for example, parenthesis, and see if the sentence would still make sense *without* the comma or commas.

CORRECT PLACING OF THE COMMA

'Now let me see, exactly where do I have to land?'

**Take care in the use of the comma.
A comma wrongly placed, or omitted, can give a sentence a meaning you did not intend.**

Examples:
The difference in meaning shown by the addition of one comma:

She is a pretty energetic girl.
She is a pretty, energetic girl.

The addition of two commas:

'Call him Charles and see whether he answers.'
'Call him, Charles, and see whether he answers.'

(a) Write out the actual note that was handed up to the priest in the following story.

During the service, a note was handed up to the priest in the pulpit. He had mislaid his spectacles but peering at the note, he read aloud:

'John Smith, having gone to see his wife, desires the prayers of the congregation for his safety.'

After the service, having found his spectacles, he glanced at the note and was dismayed to find that the word 'see' was really 'sea' and that there was only *one* comma.

'He was cross, so I said, "Well, if I called the wrong number, why did you answer the phone?"'

Speech marks inside speech marks are used when you need to quote the *actual* words spoken.

Note: You should use either double speech marks within single marks (as in the example below the illustration) or single marks inside double: " ' ... ' "

(a) Write out the following conversations, putting in the usual speech marks and *speech marks inside speech marks* where necessary.

Note: The punctuation at the end of the quoted speech should be included *inside* the speech marks of the person who spoke, as is the question mark in the example below the illustration.

1 The defendant was abusive, your Honour. When asked to clench his teeth, he took them out, gave them to the doctor and said, You clench them!

2 How did you get on at school today, dear? asked the boy's mother.
Not too well, Mum. Teacher was very annoyed with me. She said, Your composition on *My Dog* is word for word the same as your sister's composition.
And what did you say to that?
I said to her, I know, Miss – it's the same dog.

In printed books, titles of books, plays and films, are given in *italics*; in your work, you should put titles inside quotation marks.
The same rule applies to quotations of words or phrases.

Note: If the quotation is a full sentence, the first word must have *a capital letter*; this is because you are quoting the words as they were originally written.

Example:

In the book 'David Copperfield', the character of David Copperfield is based on the boyhood of Dickens.

In the same book, Mr. Micawber tells David, 'Annual income twenty pounds, annual expenditure nineteen nineteen six, result happiness.'

I have found that the remark, 'that's a good question', usually means you get a bad answer. By the time someone says, 'to cut a long story short', it's too late.

(a) Write out the following, putting in the quotation marks and *any capital letters required.*

Note: Capital letters must be used for words in titles, except for short unimportant words like: a, the, of, at, to, in, from, on, for, an, and, etc.

1 People prefer the sign no entry to the one that says no exit.

2 Wait is a hard word to the hungry.
3 I couldn't make up my mind whether to go to see the play the mouse-trap or the film the sound of music.
4 Of all the sad sayings of tongue or pen, the saddest are it might have been and we have always done it this way.
5 A drama critic was sent by his editor to see a boring play called dreadful night. He wrote a one-word review, exactly!
6 A very small spiritualist had escaped from prison. The news headline read: small medium at large!
7 During a performance of Julius Caesar, when Marc Antony declaims the speech: friends, romans, countrymen, lend me your ears..., a joker up in the balcony loudly asked what he was going to do with all those borrowed ears.

If quotation marks are used within speech, they become double quotation marks, as with the speech marks on page 12.

Examples:

'I think that I'm "undecided" but I'm not sure...'

'I've been trying to think of a word for two weeks,' said the crossword fanatic.

'How about "fortnight"?' suggested his friend.

Note the position of the question mark: it is part of the friend's comment, not part of the quotation.

(b) Write out the following with full punctuation.

1 Please miss, asked a little girl, what is a diplomat?
A diplomat, answered the teacher, is a person who, when he says yes means perhaps; when he says perhaps, he means no; when he says no, he has forgotten he is a diplomat.

2 Actually, said the beggar, I'm an author. I have written a book one hundred ways to earn money.
Then why are you begging, enquired the businessman.
It's one of the ways, replied the beggar.

3 Don't be afraid of Rover, little boy. You know the saying a barking dog never bites, don't you?
I know it and you know it, said the boy, but does the dog know it?

4 You claim you did not cheat? growled the Headmaster to the guilty-looking boy standing in front of his desk. Against the last question, the girl sitting next to you answered I don't know, and you wrote down me neither.

5 It's not the same thing a bit! said the Mad Hatter. Why you might just as well say that I see what I eat, is the same thing as I eat what I see!

6 This weighing-machine card is hilarious, said the wife.
Why, what does it say? asked her husband.
It says: you have a strong character, are intelligent, witty and attractive. It has your weight wrong, too.

7 I've found a great job. Just listen to this: good salary, free health insurance, pension scheme and long coffee-breaks.
That sounds wonderful, darling, said his admiring wife.
I knew you would be pleased.
You start on Monday.

DIRECT AND REPORTED SPEECH

**Direct speech is a report of the exact words somebody spoke (examples a. below).
Reported speech is a narrative version of what was said, written after the event (examples b. below)**

Examples of direct speech turned into reported speech:

a. 'My parents *are* in the iron and steel business,' said Tommy.
'I *know*,' said Elizabeth. 'Your mother *irons* and your father *steals*.'

b. Tommy boasted to Elizabeth that his parents *were* in the iron and steel business. Elizabeth said she *knew* that; his mother *ironed* and his father *stole*.

a. 'What *are* you doing, Mary? Learning something?' asked the teacher.
'No, sir,' replied Mary. '*I've been* listening to you.'

b. The teacher asked Mary what she *was* doing and whether she *was* learning something. Mary replied in the negative, and said that she *had been* listening to the teacher.

What changes do you notice between the two versions? Look at the speech marks and the words in italics.

1 Direct speech uses *speech marks,* because it is an actual record of the words spoken. Reported speech doesn't need speech marks, because it is a narrative record of what was said.

2 The verbs in direct speech are put into the *past tense* when reported, because the action is now over and gone.

(a) The following stories are in direct speech. Rewrite them in reported speech. You can use other words instead of 'said' for variety: for example, asked, enquired, answered, demanded, threatened, muttered, cried, etc.

1 'Your money or your life!' snarled the thief.
There was no reply.
'Your money or your life,' he repeated.
'Wait a minute,' said the old miser. 'I'm thinking it over.'

2 'As I backed out of the garage, I ran over my son's bicycle, dented my neighbour's car, and crashed into a tree.'
'Then what happened?' enquired the policeman.
'Then I lost control of the car.'

3 'I'm sorry to phone you at work, dear, but I thought I'd better tell you that the car has water in the carburettor.'
'If you'll tell me where it is,' said his wife, I'll get it seen to.'
'At the moment,' he announced, 'it's in the river.'

4 Two small boys walked straight into the dentist's surgery. The bigger boy faced him boldly and said, 'I want a tooth taken out and I don't want to have gas because I'm in a hurry.'
'I must say you're a brave boy,' said the dentist. 'Which tooth is it?'
The boy turned to his small silent companion and said, 'Show him your tooth, Albert.'

DIRECT AND REPORTED SPEECH

The smoke indicated to the Apache scout that a wagon train was coming.

5 A motorist was driving in the country when his car stopped. An old horse trotted up and said, 'Check the sparking-plugs!' The motorist was so frightened, that he ran to a nearby farmhouse and told the farmer what had happened.

'Was it an old grey horse with a flopping ear?'

'Yes! Yes!' cried the scared man.

'Pay no attention to him,' said the farmer. 'That horse knows nothing about cars.'

6 The little plane had three passengers – a boy-scout, a bishop and the Brain of Britain. The pilot turned round. 'We're out of petrol!' he shouted. 'We have only three parachutes and I'm going to take one so that I can report the crash.'

'And I must have one,' said the Brain, 'because I have so much to contribute to mankind.'
He jumped out after the pilot.

The bishop turned to the boy-scout. 'My son,' he said, 'I've had a long life; yours lies ahead. Take the last parachute – and good luck!'

'Don't worry, Bishop,' said the scout, 'we have two parachutes. The Brain of Britain has baled out with my rucksack.'

(b) When might you use direct speech in your writing, and when reported speech? What different effects do they produce?

Write down a conversation you have had today, in both styles, and compare them; then try a mixture of both direct and reported speech.

An example of *reported speech* turned into *direct speech*:

My friend, Tommy, *told* me that his dog *did not have* a nose. I *asked* how it *smelt*, and he *answered* that it *smelt* terrible.

'My dog *has* no nose,' said Tommy.
'Really?' I asked, 'then how *does* it smell?'
'It *smells* terrible!' said Tommy.

(c) The following stories are in reported speech. Write them out in the form of direct speech, using all necessary punctuation.

1 Three forest animals were arguing as to which was the most feared. The first, a hawk, claimed his prey stood no chance because he attacked from high above at great speed. The second, a lion, based his claim on his great strength and courage. The third, a skunk, proudly pointed out that he did not need speed, flight, strength or courage.

As they were discussing this, an enormous boa-constrictor (who happened to be suffering from a very severe head-cold) sprang out and swallowed them all – *hawk, lion* and *stinker.*

2 A group of young student-actors were told by their teacher to imagine that an aeroplane was taking the British Embassy staff home, before war broke out and left them stranded in a foreign country.

There was room on the plane for just one more person, and each student had to convince the armed guards that he or she had to be the one allowed on board. One after another the students made their passionate pleas, but the guards shook their heads and did not lower their guns.

Finally, one student ran up to the guards screaming that she just had to be allowed through. On being challenged by the guards as to why she should be favoured, she replied that she was the pilot.

(a) Write out the following, putting in the fifteen *capital letters* needed. Why are they used?

1 If the bank in red bank, new york buys the bank in long branch, new york, it will be called: the long branch branch of the red bank bank.

(b) Write out the following, putting in the four *apostrophes* required in each. Then write out the *full version* of each of the contractions, to show why you have used apostrophes.

2 'Wheres the dog, Charlie?'
'Im afraid Ive had him put away.'
'Was he mad?'
'Well, he wasnt exactly pleased.'

3 Doctor: 'I cant quite diagnose your complaint; I think its drink.'
Patient: 'All right, doctor, Ill come back when youre sober.'

4 Were convinced that if it werent for the optimist, the pessimist wouldnt know how happy he wasnt.

(c) Write out the following, putting in all the necessary full stops and commas for the sentences to make sense.

5 King Charles walked and talked half-an-hour after his head was cut off.

6 'Madam your dog's been chasing a man on a bicycle'
'Nonsense officer my dog can't ride a bicycle'

7 Small girl to her mother: 'Mummy I got a 100% mark today'
'Oh I am pleased what was the subject?'
'Well I had 40% in reading 30% in spelling and 30% in handwriting'

8 'Mum' said the small boy 'our class is going to be divided into two and I'm going to be in the top one I don't know who will be in the other one though it's for backward readers and no one can read backwards'

(d) Write out the following putting in the correct *hyphens.*

9 'This new hearing aid is so small that nobody notices it.'
'What kind is it?'
'Half past four.'

10 A man, limping and bent over, went to see his doctor.
'Arthritis with backache?'
'No, doctor,' said the man, 'do it yourself with paving stones.'

11 The latest candid camera for news photographers is fitted with a key hole shaped lens.

(e) Write out the following, putting in *pairs of dashes* to show parenthesis.

12 'Believe me, my young friend, there is nothing absolutely nothing half as much worth doing as simply messing about in boats.'

13 Judge: 'Did you commit this theft by yourself?'
Thief: 'Yes, your Honour you can't trust anyone these days I did it alone.'

(f) Write out the following, putting in *speech marks* and all other punctuation marks required. Remember to start a new line each time there is a change of speaker.

PUNCTUATION EXERCISES

PUNCTUATION IS
PLAIN SAILING

The comma
is a cross-wind making the boat pause for a moment.
The semi-colon
is a mooring rope holding two boats side by side.
The colon
is a boat-hook pulling one boat up to another.
The full-stop
is an anchor bringing the boat to a stop and holding it fast.

14 The young couple sat together on a park bench after a long pause she asked dreamily do you think my eyes are like stars yes he replied and do you think my teeth are like pearls she continued yes he said and do you think my hair is like spun gold in the moonlight yes he repeated oh charles she exclaimed ecstatically you say the most wonderful things.

15 In 1870 a bishop heard a scientist say one day men will fly through the air like birds the bishop angrily replied this is heresy this is blasphemy it says in the bible that flight is reserved for angels please let us have no more of such talk.

The bishop whose name was wright went home to his two small sons orville and wilbur.

(g) Write out the following, putting in the five semi-colons that are necessary.

16 What is success? To laugh often and much to win the respect of intelligent people and the affection of children to appreciate beauty to find the best in others to leave the world a little better to know even one life has breathed more easily because you lived.
This is to have succeeded.

(h) Write out the following, putting in all the necessary *capital letters, full stops* and other punctuation marks.

17 my parents placed great importance on the value of education at secondary school i was told that in order to get a good job i had to go to university i went to university when i graduated i was advised to stay on to get an honours degree as so many job applicants had the usual bachelors degree i got my honours degree after all this i was told that to get a really good job i had to get a masters degree i obtained a masters degree i was then informed that a masters degree would not get as good a job as a doctors degree
i obtained a doctors degree i started to look for a job

i started to look for a job a year ago and i am still unemployed and do you know why the employers all said i was too old

18 over a row of hooks in the school cloakroom there is a sign these hooks are for teachers only below the sign a bright spark had written they may also be used for hats and coats

Note: The sole purpose of punctuation is to clarify written work, bringing out more clearly the meaning and ideas of the writer. It is better to omit punctuation marks if they do not contribute to this purpose.

THE 'POINTING-OUT' ADJECTIVE

The demonstrative adjective points out and describes a particular noun or nouns.

For example:
this sign, *those* directions

1 *This* and *that* are used with singular nouns.

2 *These* and *those* are used with plural nouns.

(a) Write out the following, putting *this, that, these* or *those* in the blank spaces.

1 Customer: 'Has ——— dog a good pedigree?'
Salesman: 'I'll say he has. If ——— dog could talk, he wouldn't speak to either of us.'
2 'Some service, please! I want ——— dresses over there in the window.'
3 'Do ——— stairs take you the second floor?'
'No, madam, you will have to walk.'

Note: The nouns *kind* and *sort* are singular, so you must write, '*that* kind of thing', '*this* sort of thing', '*that* sort of cake', '*this* kind of book'.

The nouns *kinds* and *sorts* are plural, so you must write, '*these* kinds of books', '*those* sorts of cakes'.

THE 'POINTING-OUT' PRONOUN

The demonstrative pronoun also points out a particular noun or nouns, but it *replaces* the noun instead of *accompanying* it.

For example:
point at *this*, give me *those*

1 The demonstrative pronouns are the same words as the demonstrative adjectives, but we call them *pronouns* because they stand instead of *nouns.*

(a) Write out the following, putting *this, that, these* or *those* in the blank spaces.

1 'Waiter, this plate is wet!'
'———is your soup, sir.'
2 I have a suit for every day of the week – and ——— is the suit.
3 The biggest fish he ever caught were ———that got away.
4 'Stop, Henry! ——— isn't our baby!'
'Let's take it. ——— is a better pram.'
5 There are two types of people: ——— who divide people into types, and ———who don't.

(b) Now go through those five sentences again, turning the demonstrative *pronoun* into a demonstrative *adjective*, by adding a suitable *noun* for it to describe.

ADJECTIVES OF QUANTITY AND NUMBER

'If we can get one more in, we shall have enough to get into the Guinness Book of Records!'

What parts of speech do you think these familiar words are?
two, much, some, more, several, fewer

They are all adjectives, because they describe nouns, but they have a special name because they all deal with *amount* or *numbers*: they are called adjectives of *quantity* and *number*.

1 Here are some adjectives of *quantity*:

much, more, most; little, less, least; no; some, any; enough, sufficient; all, whole; half, quarter.

They all refer to amounts of a whole, rather than numbers of single parts.

Examples:
I don't want *any* (any quantity of) excuses. I want to hear the *whole* (the whole quantity of) truth.

As you have only a *little* (a small quantity of) money, you cannot buy *much* (a large quantity of) food.

(a) Make up five sentences of your own, using adjectives of quantity.

2 Adjectives of *number* all describe things that can be counted. They can be further divided into *definite* adjectives of number, for example:
one, two, three; first, second, third; etc.

and *indefinite* adjectives of number, for example:

All soldiers will attend parade.
No soldier will be excused.
Many soldiers are on leave.
Several soldiers are not well.
Some soldiers have gone overseas.
Few soldiers become officers.

Note: *All* is an adjective of *quantity* when it refers to an amount, and *number* when it can be counted.

(b) Make up five sentences of your own, using adjectives of number.

Note: DO NOT CONFUSE *MANY* WITH *MUCH*

Many is an adjective of quantity for things that can be counted (*many* pupils, *many* sweets, *many* motor-cars).

Much is an adjective of quantity (*much* rain, *much* food, *much* traffic).

For example:
'Never, in the field of human conflict, was so much (*amount* of gratitude) owed by so many (*number* of people) to so few (*number* again).'

MUCH IS AN AMOUNT
MANY IS USED OF A NUMBER

(c) Write out the following, putting *much* or *many* in the blank spaces.

1 It never troubles the wolf how ——— sheep there may be.
2 Optician: I don't think there's ——— wrong with your eyes. How ——— lines can you read on that chart?
Customer: What chart?

POSSESSIVE ADJECTIVES

THE 'OWNERSHIP' ADJECTIVE

What parts of speech are these words:
my, his, her, its, our, your and their?

1 Again, they are adjectives, but because each of them describes an example of *ownership*, they are called *possessive* adjectives.

(a) Fill in the gaps with: *my, his, her, its, our, your* and *their.* Then underline the noun which the possessive adjective *describes.*

An example:
Father glow-worm to mother: '——— son is bright for his age, isn't he?'
Father glow-worm to mother: 'Our son is bright for his age, isn't he?'

1 One morning, in the jungle, I shot an elephant in ——— pyjamas. How he got into my pyjamas, I shall never know.
2 'Have ——— eyes been checked?'
'No sir, they've always been brown.'
3 First small boy: '——— father can beat ——— father.'
Second small boy: 'I wouldn't be surprised; so can ——— mother.'
4 'What's the time? I'm invited to dinner at 8.30 and ——— watch isn't going.'
'Why? Wasn't ——— watch invited?'
5 Fat woman: 'On the bus, today, three men offered me ——— seats.'
Thin woman: 'And did you take them?'
6 'I hear she broke off ——— engagement to John. What happened?'
'———feelings towards him changed.'
'Is she returning ——— ring?'
'No, ——— feelings towards the ring haven't changed a bit.'
7 '——— wife doesn't appreciate me. How about ——— wife?'
'I wouldn't know. I've never heard her mention ——— name.'
8 'Why do you two have carrots sticking out of ——— ears?'
'We can't hear you. We have carrots sticking out of ——— ears.'
9 The first half of people's lives is ruined by ——— parents, and the second half is ruined by ——— children.
10 A teacher warned her infant pupils never to kiss ——— pet animals.
'But miss,' said one small girl, 'my two aunties used to kiss ——— dog.'
'And what happened?'
'It died.'
11 'I've been feeding ——— dog garlic.'
'What on earth for?'
'To make sure its bark is worse than ——— bite'.
'Why is it staring at me like that?'
'You're eating from ——— dish,

Note: Care must be taken to avoid confusing the possessive adjective *its* (without an apostrophe) and the word *it's* (with an apostrophe).

It's represents the two words *it is* (or the two words *it has*); the two words have been brought together and shortened by the use of an apostrophe. For example:
'What's up with your dog? *It's* (*it is*) staring at me!'
'Well, you're eating from *its* dish.'

The possessive adjective *its* goes with the noun *dish,* which it describes; it would not be possible to say '*it is dish*', therefore no apostrophe applies.

POSSESSIVE PRONOUNS

'THESE BONES ARE OURS!'

THE 'OWNERSHIP' PRONOUN

The possessive pronouns also refer to examples of ownership, but as they *replace* nouns instead of *accompanying* them we call them possessive *pronouns*.

For example:
This book is *mine*.
(instead of *my book*)

Yours is the true answer.
(instead of *your answer*)

That son of *ours* is bright.
(instead of *our son*)

This coat is *his*.
(instead of *his coat*)

That handbag is *hers*.
(instead of *her handbag*)

The clothes are *theirs*.
(instead of *their clothes*)

(a) Write out the following, putting possessive pronouns in the blank spaces.

1 Father glow-worm to mother: 'That son of ——— is bright for his age.'
2 'My eyes have been checked. Have ———?'
'No, they've always been brown.'
3 'My wife doesn't appreciate me. Does ———?'
'I wouldn't know. I've never heard her mention your name.'
4 Few women admit their age. Very few men act ———.
5 If you wish others to keep your secrets, you must keep ———.
6 Teacher: 'Johnny, these answers of ———: were you copying from Mary?'
Johnny: 'No, miss, I was only looking to see if she had ——— right.'
7 'It must be a bore shaving your face. Do you shave ——— all the time?
'No, I stop occasionally for food.'
8 A woman got on a bus with seven children. The conductor asked, 'Are these all ———, lady, or is it a picnic?'
'They are all ———,' came the tired reply, 'and it's no picnic.'
9 'You stick to your washing, ironing, scrubbing and cooking,' a husband told his wife. 'No wife of ——— is going to work!'
10 'Haven't you ever had a quarrel with your wife?'
'Never. She goes her way, and if she lets me, I go ———.'

Note: The possessive pronouns (with the exception of *mine*) end with the letter 's'. You must never put an apostrophe in front of the 's' of a possessive pronoun.

Note the difference between:
theirs (a possessive pronoun) and
there's (the shortened form of the two words *there is* or *there has*)

You will sometimes use a noun or name rather than a possessive pronoun. To indicate that the noun or name is possessive, you add 's to the end. For example:
This house is *Elizabeth's*.
This is your duty, not *your employer's*.

(b) Make up five sentences of your own, using the possessive form of a name in the above style.

REFLEXIVE PRONOUNS

'Why are you scratching yourself?'
'Me sir? I'm the only one who knows where it itches.'

The reflexive pronoun is used to refer back ('reflect' back) to someone earlier in the sentence.

Singular reflexive pronouns:
myself, yourself, himself, herself, itself

Plural reflexive pronouns:
ourselves, yourselves, themselves
(there is no such word as 'theirselves' – the correct word is '*themselves*')

Note that the reflexive pronoun makes it clear that the 'doer' of the action *is the same person* as the 'receiver' of it.

He stopped *himself* from smoking.

(a) Write out the following, putting *myself, yourself, himself, herself* or *itself* in the spaces.

1 Psychiatrist: 'What's your problem, my friend?'
Santa Claus: 'I don't believe in ———.'
2 A candle lights others and consumes ———.
3 Don't talk about ———; everyone else will do so when you leave the room.
4 They are madly in love, he with ———, she with ———.
5 Salesmanship is a puppy selling ——— to a small boy.
6 The person who says he trusts no one, should include ———.
7 If she could see ——— as others see her, she would never want to take a second look.
8 Judge: 'I am going to give your wife £200 a month alimony.'
Husband: 'Thanks, your Honour. I'll try to give her something ———.'
9 Husband: 'Your brother is the loudest-mouthed man I ever heard!'
Wife: 'Shush, dear, you forget ———.'
10 A gossip talks to you about others; a bore talks to you about ———; a brilliant speaker is one who talks to you about ———.

(b) Write out the following, putting *ourselves, yourselves* or *themselves* in the spaces.

1 Notice on greengrocer's display: 'God helps those who help ———!'
2 'Be men! Make ——— lambs and the wolves will eat you.'
3 No secret is harder to keep than our good opinion of ———.
4 Sign inside a restaurant:
'Our tongue sandwiches speak for ———.'
5 It is easy to see through people who make a 'spectacle' of ———.'
6 Nothing makes it harder for us to be on good terms with others than being ill at ease with ———.
7 I know a hostess who likes to pour custard herself over the pudding before serving, but I prefer to let my guests pour it over ———.

(c) Write out five sentences of your own, using reflexive pronouns.

Note: A reflexive pronoun cannot be used as the subject of a verb. For example: '*My husband and myself went home*' is incorrect, because it says: 'My husband went home and *myself* went home.' The correct sentence should be: 'My husband and *I* went home.'

EMPHATIC PRONOUNS

'I myself am looking at you.'

The emphatic pronouns are the same words as the reflexive pronouns, but they are used differently.

The emphatic pronoun is used only for *emphasis*, so it can be taken away and the sentence will *still make sense.*

An example, using 'itself' first as emphatic pronoun:
'The cat *itself* cleaned its kittens.'

Even without the emphatic pronoun this would still make sense, i.e.
'The cat cleaned its kittens.'

then as a reflexive pronoun:

'The cat cleaned *itself*.'

Without the reflexive pronoun (*'The cat cleaned'*) the above sentence would not make sense.

(a) Write out the following, with *emphatic pronouns* for emphasis.

1 If parents want honest children, they ——— must be honest.
2 A comedian loses some of the joke when he ——— joins in the laughter of the audience.

SUITABLE ADJECTIVES

Adjectives which are 'worn-out' through having been used too much should be avoided. Adjectives which are powerful should be reserved for the few occasions when their use will create a powerful effect of style.

(a) The following letter from a girl to her friend has been written unimaginatively with rather overworked adjectives. Write the letter again, replacing the adjectives in italics with more imaginative words.

Dear Mary,
On Saturday, I went to see the Rolling Bones Pop Group; it was *super sensational*!
The singing was really *great* and they all looked *gorgeous,* especially the leader, who was *smashing* in his *stupendous* costume. I thought the disco-lighting was *tremendous,* with *fabulous* staging.
It was a *fantastic* show, although for the *horrendous* price of the tickets, I thought the hard seats *pretty horrific.*
I had a *nice* evening.
Susan

ACTIVE & PASSIVE VERBS

'I am the active verb; I perform the action done to the subject.'

An example:
'The lion *beat* the unicorn.'

> **Verbs may be divided into the active or passive 'voice'.**
> **If the subject of a sentence is the 'doer' of the action, the verb is *active*.**
> **If the subject of a sentence is the 'receiver' of the action, the verb is *passive*.**

The active voice of the verb is *stronger* and *more direct* than the passive voice. Because the active is usually shorter and easier to read, *it is used much more often* than the passive.

Examples of the active verb:
The dog *bites* the postman.
The dog *bit* the postman.
The dog *will bite* the postman.

Examples of the passive verb:
The postman *is bitten* by the dog.
The postman *was bitten* by the dog.
The postman *will be bitten* by the dog.

'I am the passive verb; I receive the action done to the subject.'

An example:
'The unicorn *was beaten* by the lion.'

The passive voice can give quite a different emphasis to your written sentences.

Public notices, for example, are usually in the *passive* voice because the *active* might seem to be tactless and abrupt, for example:
'SMOKING IS NOT PERMITTED' (passive)
is better than
'DO NOT SMOKE!' (active)

(a) Write out the following, changing the active into the passive voice.

1. Notice: 'We Prosecute Thieves!'
2. Notice: 'Carry small children and dogs on this escalator.'
3. Elizabeth is cooking the supper.
4. The opening batsman scored a six.
5. The Germans invaded Poland in 1939.
6. You must complete and return the application form immediately.
7. Give your train tickets to the collector when you leave the station.
8. The little girl ate up all her supper and pleased her mother.
9. I once discovered a certain cure for amnesia but I can't remember it.
10. I took my mongrel dog to a flea circus and it stole the show.

(b) Make up five sentences, using a verb in the active voice in each one.

(c) Make up five sentences, using a verb in the passive voice in each one.

TRANSITIVE & INTRANSITIVE VERBS

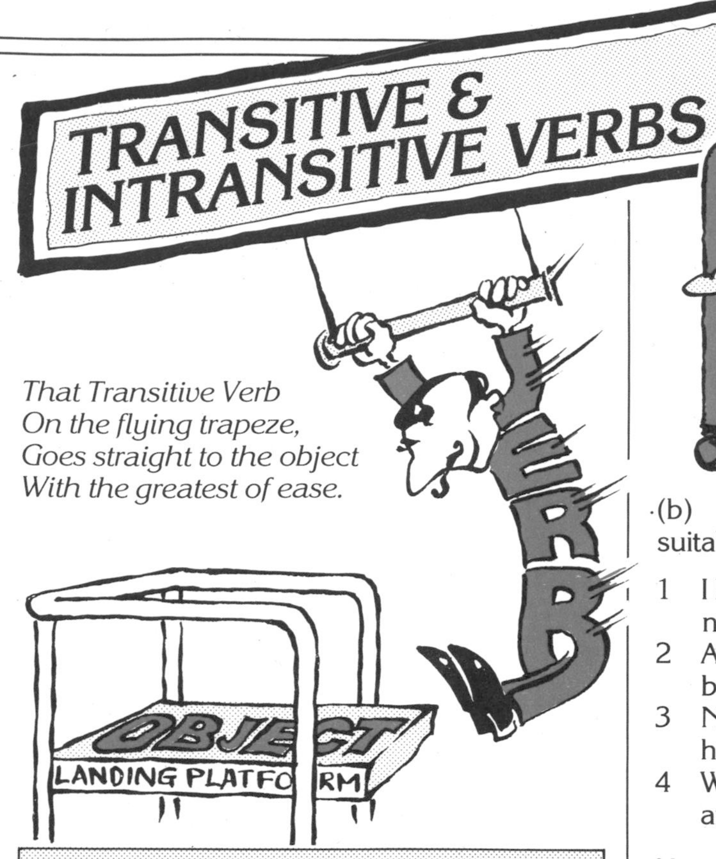

That Transitive Verb
On the flying trapeze,
Goes straight to the object
With the greatest of ease.

Intransitive patient
– Do not disturb!
Make sure that no object
Gets near to this verb

A *transitive* verb is one in which an action is done by *the subject* of the sentence to *the object*.
An *intransitive* verb is one in which there is *no object*.

For example:
The cat (subject) chased (transitive verb) the mouse (object).
The dog (subject) barked (intransitive verb).
(The dog can't *bark something*.)

(a) Write out the following, putting in suitable *transitive* verbs.

1 Elizabeth settled down and ——— the newspaper.
2 The hunter ——— the leopard.
3 The children have gone to the open fields to ——— their kites.
4 If you ——— the candle at both ends it helps to read the menu.
5 'Are these eggs fresh?'
'Fresh? Why, madam, these eggs are so fresh, the hens haven't ——— them yet.'

(b) Write out the following, putting in suitable *intransitive* verbs.

1 I have chosen the present I want, and now it is your turn to ———.
2 A kitten is born blind, but a new-born baby ———.
3 Nocturnal animals ——— during day-light hours.
4 When it hears a cat, a mouse is silent and ——— in its hole.

Note: There are many verbs which can be either transitive or intransitive, depending upon how they are used in the sentence.

For example:
The referee separated (transitive) the boxers.

After only two years of marriage, the husband and wife separated (intransitive verb).

(c) Write out the following, and after the words *sing* and *play* put in brackets either *transitive* or *intransitive* according to use.

Elizabeth: 'What do the angels do in heaven, Mummy?'
Mother: 'They *sing* and *play*.'
Elizabeth: 'What do they *sing* and *play*, Mummy?'
Mother: 'I suppose they *sing* hymns and *play* harps.'
Elizabeth: 'Why don't they just put on the radio?'
Mother: 'Very funny! Now go into the garden and *play*.'
Elizabeth: 'May I *play* football?'
Mother: 'You may *play* what you please as long as you don't *play* on my nerves.'

Book 1 showed that adverbs give more meaning to the verb by saying *how, when* or *where* the action happens.

The adverb of *manner* tells *how* an action is done, for example:
The athlete ran (verb) *quickly*.

The adverb of *time* tells *when* an action is done, for example:
Yesterday I lost (verb) my pen.

The adverb of *place* tells *where* an action is done, for example:
No one stays (verb) *here*.

The adverb of degree tells to what extent (or degree) the action takes place. The other adverbs tell more about the *verb*; the adverb of degree tells more about an *adjective* or another *adverb*.

Example:
We saw a *very* old (adjective) church.

The athlete ran *very* quickly (adverb).

This book is *more* interesting (adjective) than that one.

This book is the *most* interesting (adjective) one I have ever read,

That hat is *too* small (adjective) for your head.

They arrived much *too* soon (adverb).

To train your dog well, you should praise *rather* loudly (adverb) and scold *extremely* sternly (adverb).

You will always stay young if you live *completely* honestly (adverb), eat *fairly* sensibly (adverb), sleep *quite* sufficiently (adverb), work *really* industriously (adverb), and above all – tell lies about your age!

(a) Write out the following, underlining all the adverbs of degree. For example :

'How should you dress on a freezing-cold morning?'
'Very swiftly.'

1 'How far is it to the next town?'
'Five miles. You can walk it quite easily in an hour, if you run.'
2 'That horse you sold me is almost blind!'
'I told you he was a good horse but he didn't look good.'
3 'I hear your daughter speaks Esperanto. Does she speak it really fluently?'
'Fluently enough to be taken for a native.'
4 'Heads I win – tails, you lose,' the boy said somewhat flippantly.
5 'Good morning, Reverend. And is this your most charming wife?'
'This, sir, is my only wife!'
6 Customer: 'Young man, have you anything for grey hair?'
Chemist: 'Nothing, madam, but the most deep respect.'
7 On the surface he seems fairly deep, but deep down he is completely shallow.

(b) Write out a few sentences of your own, containing underlined adverbs of degree. Here are a few examples you might use:

partly, utterly, mainly, just, slightly, entirely, exceedingly.

Note: Some adverbs of degree may be used to modify *verbs*, for example:

I *quite* sympathize.
You *hardly* know me.
The ball *nearly* hit me.

Adverbs which are 'worn-out' or are useless because they add nothing to the sentence should be avoided.

Here is a letter to a bishop, giving examples of useless adverbs which make the adjectives *less* effective:

Your Grace,
It was so *absolutely* good of you to send our tribe a missionary. We found him *awfully* kind, *terribly* considerate, *fantastically* clever and *superbly* delicious.
Yours sincerely,
The Cannibal Chief

(a) Write out the letter, leaving out the useless adverbs of degree.

Some good adverbs are spoiled by being used incorrectly. Note how they are used *wrongly* in a. and *correctly* in b.:

a. I must *definitely* get some sleep.
b. The doctor told me to give up smoking cigarettes or I would *definitely* develop lung-cancer.

a. The angry man *literally* exploded.
b. There is *literally* nothing to eat.

a. *Hopefully* I will see you tomorrow.
b. Billy Bunter was always *hopefully* expecting to get a postal-order.

(b) Write out a few sentences of your own, using the above adverbs in a correct and useful manner.

Make sure that adverbs are placed correctly, to avoid any possible confusion or unintended meaning. *Only* is particularly important.

For example:
I can lend you *only* £10.
(Placed next to *£10*, the word *only* states the maximum amount of the loan.)

I can *only* lend you £10.
(Placed next to *lend*, the world *only* then means that a loan is possible but not a gift.)

As a general rule, the adverb should be placed *as close as possible* to the word to which it relates.

(a) In your own words, give the two different meanings of the following:

A king can create a lord, but *only* God can make a gentleman.
A king can create a lord, but God can *only* make a gentleman.

(b) Write out the following, putting the word *only* in the appropriate place:

1 Locks keep out the honest citizen.
2 'Does the fire in the kitchen mean there's cheese for dinner?'
3 I quote other writers the better to express my own ideas.

The dog is near (preposition) the cat.

A preposition is a word used to show the position of one thing in relation to another.

These are some common prepositions:

in on of for
from with up down
above below before after
over under into until
behind beneath beyond beside
around against along across
among between through near

Examples of prepositions in use:
The bird is *in* the nest.
The boy climbed *up* the steep hill.
The girl is studying *at* college.
The train went *through* the tunnel.
She took her sister *with* her.
It was very early *in* the morning.
She walked slowly *into* the pool.
I have no time *for* arguing with you.
She emerged *from behind* (two prepositions) the curtains.

(a) Select a few prepositions from the list at the top, and put them into sentences of your own.

(b) Write out the following, underlining the prepositions.

Example:
Some people don't know the difference between thinking for yourself and thinking of yourself.

1 'Hello, old man, why the smile of satisfaction on your face?'
'I've just got a bottle of whisky for the wife.'
'That sounds a fair swop.'

2 What did the male owl tell the female owl in the pouring rain?
'It's too wet to woo.'

3 He who is a judge between two friends loses one of them.

4 That man is so lucky! Throw him into the river and he will come up with a fish in his mouth.

5 The husband was in the habit of gossiping with friends and coming home from work so late that his wife decided to teach him a lesson. She left him a note on the table: 'Your dinner is in the dog!'

6 An old lady ran to help a man who seemed to be floating down from the dark storm-swept sky.
'You're a silly young man to go parachuting on a night like this!'
'I'm not coming down by parachute, lady, I'm going up with a tent!'

7 'Sir, I would like to be allowed to marry your daughter.'
'Nonsense, young man. My daughter will get married by a proper vicar.'
'You misunderstand me, sir; I want your daughter for my wife.'
'Silly man, what would your wife want with my daughter around the place?'
The young man left in a hurry; he was scared the girl might have inherited her father's intelligence.

8 'I hear your husband is in hospital. What's wrong with him?'
'He's suffering from fallen arches.'
'I didn't know he had bad feet.'
'He hasn't. A railway bridge fell on him.'

ADVERB OR PREPOSITION?

Some words may be used as adverbs or prepositions depending on the context.

Examples:
He *took* (verb) the dog *inside* (adverb).
The word *inside* has been used as an adverb linked to *took*.

He took the *dog* (noun) *inside* (preposition) the *house* (noun).
The word *inside* has been used as a preposition linking *dog* and *house*.

(a) Write out the following, putting *adverb* or *preposition* after each word in italics.

'Do you see that fellow, Sergeant? He lives *down* those stairs *in* a very narrow room.'

'Really, Inspector? How *on* earth can you deduce that?'

'His dog wags his tail *up* and *down* instead of sideways. I noticed it when he walked *past* us at half-*past* three, *with* his dog trotting *behind*. We were hiding *behind* the door waiting for the suspect to arrive so that we could go *across* to that shop *across* the street and arrest him.'

THE PAST PARTICIPLE

The past participle and the present participle (see page 30) are so called because they *participate* as a form of the verb.

The past participle is the part of the verb which follows 'have' in the past tense, for example:

They have *spoken*.
It has been *sung*.
I have *written*.
(The second example is in the passive.)

These past participles can then be used as adjectives as well as forms of a verb, for example:

In ancient times, stories consisted only of the *spoken* word.
After many years, the stories were made into *sung* versions.
Later still, scribes produced an alphabet and *written* stories appeared.

(a) Write out the following, putting suitable past participles in the blank spaces, and in brackets indicate whether they are being used as a verb or an adjective.

Example:
If you want to stop drinking, look at a *drunken* (adjective) man when you are sober.

1 The man who has been ——— by a snake is afraid of a piece of rope.
2 My boy-friend is a man of rare gifts. He hasn't ——— a gift to me in years.
3 'Please, miss, what is this ——— remark in my book?'
'In future, write more clearly!'
4 I wasn't able to give my lecture on 'Amnesia' because of a ——— appointments book.
5 'Doctor, my baby has ——— a flash-bulb and has ——— the film out of the camera.'
'Don't worry, madam. Keep him in a dark room and see what develops.'

THE PRESENT PARTICIPLE

William Tell was an archer famous for his shooting *skill.*
Gessler told Tell to prove his skill by aiming *an arrow at an apple perched on the head of Tell's small son.*
Tell told me the story and now I am telling *the story to you.*

The present participle is the part of the verb that ends in *-ing*, for example: roaring, dripping, laughing, dancing.
It can be used as either a *verb*, an *adjective* or a *noun*.

1 Examples of the present participle used as a *verb* (usually helped by an auxiliary verb):

The fire was *roaring* fiercely.
I wish the tap would stop *dripping*.
The children are *laughing* and *dancing* as they follow the band.

Note: In spite of its name, the present participle is not limited to the present tense of the verb. For example: 'She was *brushing* her hair', or 'She *will be brushing* her hair'. The same form of participle is used each time for a description of *continuous action*, while the auxiliary verb indicates the past, present or future tense.

2 Examples of the present participle used as an *adjective*:

We sat in front of a *roaring* fire.
A *dripping* tap can be annoying.
The band was followed by a *laughing* group of *dancing* children.

Spelling note:
When *-ing* is added to a word ending in the silent letter *-e*, the *-e* is usually omitted, for example:

dance	danc*ing*
balance	balanc*ing*

When *-ing* is added to a word with a short vowel followed by a *single* consonant, the consonant is *doubled*, for example:

dri*p*	dri*pp*ing
pa*d*	pa*dd*ing

(a) Write out the following, underlining present participles used as *verbs*.

Example:
'Are you <u>fishing</u> the stream?'
'No, I'm just <u>drowning</u> a few worms.'

1. Conscience is the inner voice that tells us someone is watching.
2. The final test of fame is, after you are dead, to have some crazy man go around imagining he is you.
3. Small girl to Scotsman playing the bagpipes: 'If you let it go, maybe it will stop screaming.'
4. A photographer whose speciality was taking portraits is now in prison. He was caught taking one from the National Portrait Gallery.

(b) Write out the following, underlining any present participles used as *adjectives,* and then naming the noun that adjective describes.

Example:
A man without a <u>smiling</u> face should not open a shop. (face)

1. Customer: 'Your opening sale has closed. What happens now?'
   Assistant: 'Our closing sale opens.'
2. 'Who said barking dogs don't bite? Just look at my trousers!'
3. Let sleeping dogs lie.
4. A rolling stone gathers no moss.

THE PRESENT PARTICIPLE AS NOUN

THE BARKING OF THE DOG

3 The third use of the present partciple is as a *noun*.

For example:
The *roaring* of the fire.
The *dripping* got on my nerves.
My *laughing* meant the end of the *dancing*.
The *barking* of the dog.
When the present participle is used as a noun in this way, it is properly called a *gerund*.

You will find a number of *gerunds* in this well-known Christmas carol:

The *rising* of the sun
And the *running* of the deer,
The *playing* of the merry organ,
Sweet *singing* in the choir.

You should be able to tell when the present participle is acting as a gerund, because *it behaves as an ordinary noun:* try putting the words 'the action of' before a present participle, and if that makes sense it must be a gerund.
For example:
Losing is more fun when you are *fighting* temptation.
('The action of losing', but *not* 'you are the action of fighting'.
Losing is acting as a gerund; *fighting* is acting as a verb.)

Also, since the gerund is a noun, you say '*my* winning' and '*his* losing', not 'me winning' and him losing'. These are *possessive adjectives* (refer to page 20).

GERUND IS A VERBAL NOUN

The following sentences give examples of correct use:

I was praised for *my* singing. (NOT I was praised for me singing.)

Leave without *his* knowing. (NOT leave without him knowing.)

(c) Write out the following, underlining all the gerunds.

1 Fishing is my favourite sport.
2 I do not like Tom's being appointed.
3 They watched our launching the boat.
4 A good book traps the mind into doing its own thinking.
5 'Why do wild geese always fly south?'
'Walking would take too long.'
6 'Are you familiar with the saying: "Understanding is forgiving"?'

(d) Write out the following, and after each present participle state whether it is being used as a verb, adjective or noun.

For example:
'The barking (noun) of that dog chasing (verb) the cat is annoying (verb) me.'
'Me too. And that barking (adjective) dog is barking (verb) up the wrong tree, anyway.'

1 'This must be a good hunting spot.'
'Yes, the sign says: "Fine for Hunting".'
2 'You naughty boy! Pulling the cat's tail is spiteful and cruel!'
'But Mum, I'm only holding it. The cat is doing the pulling.'
3 Park-keeper: 'Hey, you! Can't you read the notice: "Swimming Prohibited"?'
'I'm not swimming . . . I'm drowning!'
Keeper: 'Oh, that's all right then.'

CORRECT USE OF THE PRESENT PARTICIPLE

'As far as I can make out, it says "'Scribes must pay particular attention to the correct use of the participle."'

The present participle is the part of the verb that ends in -ing (see pages 30 and 31). If it is not put in the correct place, the sentence will not mean what you want it to.

1 Look at the difference between these two sentences:

Going home, James met his friends.
James met his friends going home.

If you put 'going home' near James, it refers to him; if you put 'going home' near the friends, it refers to them. Always think about where to place your present participle, therefore, in order to make your meaning clear.

2 There is also a rule that the present participle refers to the *subject* of the sentence unless otherwise indicated. So, if you say:

'Sitting on a farmyard gate, a goat gave me a butt with his horns.'

you are saying that the goat is sitting on the gate. You must therefore be more specific:

'While I was sitting on a farmyard gate, a goat gave me a butt with his horns.'

3 Finally, make sure you use the correct pronoun when the present participle is used as a verbal noun (see page 31). Do not say:
'I don't like *you* coming home late.'
You should say:
'I don't like *your* coming home late.'

(a) Write out the following, correcting the errors caused by:
incorrect placing of the present participle;
omitted or incorrect subject of the sentence;
use of the wrong pronoun.

1 Grunting happily, the farmer gave out food and water to his pigs.
2 Dashing through the room at full speed, the table got in his way.
3 While waiting for the kettle to boil, the toast was burnt.
4 I noticed your smart new carpet, coming downstairs.
5 Being unable to contact the fire brigade, the fire destroyed the house.
6 Mourning and weeping with grief, the dead man was placed in his coffin.
7 While sitting there quietly, the stage suddenly exploded with gaity.
8 Sitting drowsily in the sun, reading a magazine, a large black cat rubbed against my legs.
9 The men sit huddled together as the blizzard passes over them wondering how long it will last.
10 Warning shots were fired, and, after travelling many miles at high speed, a bullet pierced a rear-tyre of the stolen car.
11 'Is there danger of him being hurt?'
12 'He invited her to the house without me knowing.'
13 'Do you mind us coming with you?'
14 'It was him scoring the final goal that brought us victory.'
15 'Them winning the game delighted the cheering supporters.'
16 The explorer was injured after a hippopotamus charged at him while rowing a small boat on the river.

PRACTICE & PRACTISE, ETC.

PRACTICE IS A
COMMON NOUN
LICENCE IS A
COMMON NOUN

PRACTISE AND LICENSE ARE VERBS

Examples:
The pupils do their piano *practice* ('practice' is a common noun) on Saturdays. They *practise* ('practise' is a verb) the piano for at least two hours.

To use a television-set you are obliged to pay for a *licence* ('licence' is a common noun). It costs more to *license* ('license' is a verb) a colour T.V. than a black-and-white television.

(a) Write out the following, putting *practice, practise, licence* or *license* in the blank spaces.

1 The small girl was talking about the recent fire in her school.
'I knew it was going to happen,' she said, 'because we've had lots of ——— for it all year, and teacher told us that you have to ——— to make perfect.'

2 'Good morning! I would like to take out a dog ———, please.'
'Certainly, sir. What name?'
'Fido.'
'Then please ask Fido to pay the fee to ——— the dog.'

3 The paratroopers were ready to ——— their first jump. The last man came forward.
'Stop!' shouted the sergeant. 'You're not wearing your parachute!'
'Oh, that's all right, sarge,' he smiled, 'You said it was only a ——— jump.'

'It's quite easy, son, with practice; you should practise first on a chair.'

Similarly, *advice* is a noun, *advise* is a verb. If you say them out loud, you can actually hear the difference between -ice and -ise.

(b) Write out the following, putting *Advice* or *advise* in the spaces.

1 Teacher: 'Why was Solomon the wisest man in the whole world?'
Pupil: 'Because he had so many wives to ——— him and they gave him very good ———.'

2 Motorist: 'I would like you to ——— me about changing the oil in my car.
Mechanic: 'My ——— is that you keep the oil and change the car.'

(c) In the following paragraph, the letters 'c' and 's' have been omitted. Rewrite the paragraph putting in the missing letters.

My father is a solicitor with a *practi-e* in the High Street and he has a *licen-e* to *practi-e* law. He has been *practi-ing* now for about five years and gives *advi-e* on the *licen-ing* laws relating to premises *licen-ed* to sell alcohol and tobacco. He is prepared to *advi-e* anyone with a problem and spends time with business men *advi-ing* them how to cut their costs.

Note: If you should happen to read newspapers, magazines or books printed in the United States, you will notice that this rule 'C for a noun – S for a verb' is reversed in that country.

PASSED IS A VERB
PAST IS NOT A VERB

'Mummy, Daddy just fell off the roof!'
'I know, dear; I saw him as he passed.'

Passed may only be used as a *verb.*

Past may be used as an *adjective*
(the past month; in time past)
Past may be used as a *noun*
(the good times of the past)
Past may be used as an *adverb*
(try to hurry past; hasten past)
Past may be used as a *preposition*
(ran past the house; half past two)

(a) Write out the following, putting *passed* or *past* in the spaces.

1. 'I'm not sure if this verb is in the ——— tense or is a ——— participle.'
2. Father Time controls the future as well as the ———; he walks by your side, but he has not ——— you yet.
3. Employer: 'On your way to Smith & Sons, you go ——— a football ground.'
   Office-boy (hopefully): 'Yes, sir!'
   Employer: 'Well, make sure you go on ———, and not inside.'
4. She walked ——— me without looking, and on her way back, she ——— me again. Really, it is quite ——— belief!

(b) Each time you have used 'past', say whether it was an adjective, a noun, an adverb or a preposition.

'Silence is quite golden,
No one can deny it:
Why won't those cats just leave us
To sit in peace and quiet?'

Quiet is an *adjective* meaning 'with little or no sound'.

Quite is an *adverb* meaning 'completely', 'altogether'.

They are actually pronounced differently, and you spell them as they sound.

For example:
No one is *quite* (meaning 'completely') so busy as the *quiet* (meaning 'making little sound') man who works steadily.

(a) Write out the following, putting *quiet* or *quite* in the spaces.

1. Teacher: 'What three words are most used in this classroom?'
   Pupil: 'I don't know.'
   Teacher: '——— correct!'
2. 'Didn't the burglar wake you up?'
   'No, he took things quietly. He was really ——— ——— and considerate.'
3. 'It's very ——— sir, too ———; I don't like it!'
   'Go to sleep, soldier; everything's ——— all right. Personally, I ——— like it when it's all ———; it means we're ——— safe from the enem... .'

DEPENDENT & DEPENDANT

I AM
DEPENDENT
ON YOUR KIND
CHARITY TO
SUPPORT MY
DEPENDANTS

The fiddler above is saying that he is *dependent* (adjective) on people giving him money to help his *dependants* (noun).

You might be depend*ent* (adjective) on someone else for support, for example:
This family is *dependent* on the mother's weekly wages.

Or you might be a depend*ant* (noun) of someone else, for example:
His only *dependant* is his aged mother.

(a) Write out the following, putting *dependent* or *dependant(s)* in the blank spaces.

1 The success of the sports-day is largely ——— on the weather.
2 If you have a ——— the amount of income tax you pay is reduced.
3 Young people want to earn their own living as soon as possible in order not to be ——— on their parents.
4 Reference books are useful, but you should not become too ——— on them.
5 Dependants are ——— on the person whose ——— they are.
6 'Did you have a good day at the office dear?' 'Terrible! You know how ——— I am on our computer which works out the allowances for ———? Well, it broke down today, and I had to think.'

PRINCIPLE & PRINCIPAL

PRINCIPLE...IS A NOUN
PRINCIPAL...IS AN ADJECTIVE

Examples:
The human eye works on the same *principle* (noun) as a camera.

A *principle* (noun) is a law or rule of action.

The *principal* (adjective) witness in the case was given special protection by the police.

Exception: Occasionally the noun following the adjective *principal* is omitted, but it still remains an adjective, for example:
The Principal of the College
(the principal *teacher* of the College)

(a) Write out the following, putting *principle(s)* or *principal* in the blank spaces.

1 It is easier to fight for one's ——— than to live up to them.
2 She acted in the pantomime as the ——— boy.
3 The ——— of geometry are not easy to master.
4 The ——— task of the lawyer was to set out the ——— of the law.
5 The ——— of our college believes in ——— before practice.
6 I am different from George Washington; I have a higher standard of ———. Washington could not tell a lie. I can lie, but I won't.

AS & LIKE

As is followed by a *verb*.
(She sings *as* you *do*).
Like is followed by a *noun* or *pronoun* only.
(She sings *like* you).

For example:
Millions saw the apple fall, but Newton asked the question 'why?':

be observant *as* Newton *was* (verb)
be observant *like Newton* (noun)

(a) Write out the following, putting *as* and *like* in the blank spaces.

1 'I'll never forget the day I was born. I cried ——— a baby.'
2 'Boy! Stop acting ——— a fool!'
'Please sir, I'm not acting.'
3 Angry mother to small son:
'You shouldn't ask me for 50p for being good; you should be good for nothing ——— your father.'
4 'I want you to read your book quietly ——— I told you to do, ——— a good little boy.'
5 Mary swam ——— a champion, and won the race incredibly easily ——— she did last year.
6 After we had done the revision ——— we were told, we worked on the problems ——— the teacher had previously shown us.
7 Bill took a shot at goal ——— Tom did, with a kick ——— that of an enraged donkey.

FEWER & LESS

FEWER IS FOR NUMBER

Fewer means 'smaller in number' and is applied to people or objects that can be *counted* as individual units.

Less means 'smaller in amount' and is applied to objects or abstract nouns that are *measured* in bulk.

Examples:
I drink *fewer* cups of tea than I used to.
(*number* of cups)
I drink *less* tea than I used to.
(tea taken as an *amount*, not in units)

Fewer people use trains.
(Never say 'less people', because people are always counted in this sense as numbers of individuals.)

(a) Write out the following, putting *less* or *fewer* in the spaces.

1 The more arguments you win, the ——— friends you will have.
2 We have two ears and one mouth so that we may listen the more and talk the ———.
3 If people would think more, they would act ——— and do ——— foolish things.
4 The deeper the grief the ——— words can express it. The deeper the grief, the ——— the words that can express it.

DISINTERESTED & UNINTERESTED
Do not confuse disinterested with uninterested: the two words have very different meanings

Disinterested means impartial, without commitment to either side:
Uninterested simply means without any interest at all.
For example:
The Judge in court dispenses justice impartially and without bias; he or she is *interested* in each case, but is *disinterested* in the outcome.

If judges were to be bored or sleepy during the case, they would be *uninterested*, i.e. not showing any *interest*, unlikely though this might be.

(a) Write out the following, putting *uninterested* or *disinterested* in the blank spaces, as required.

1 The Secretary works hard for the Sports Club, but he will always be a ——— official because he is unpaid.
2 The Trade Union and the Employers agreed to take their dispute to an independent arbitrator and accept that person's ——— decision.
3 Although he was ——— in legal matters, he agreed to be an executor of the will. As he himself was left nothing in the will, he was a very suitable person to undertake the task because he was quite ———.

IF IT'S IMPLIED – IT'S SPOKEN
IF IT'S INFERRED – IT'S HEARD

The speaker (or writer) hints, insinuates, or *implies*.
The listener (or reader) draws a conclusion, or *infers*.

Example:
I have heard that person (the speaker) *imply* that when people laugh a great deal, they are happy.
I disagree. I (the listener) *infer* from excessive laughter that people are really sad.

(a) Write out the following, putting *imply, implies, infer* or *infers* in the blank spaces.

1 'It says here that the Police are trying hard to stop gambling.'
'That is badly written; it ——— that the Police are gamblers.'
2 'I want you to keep that dog out of the house – it's full of fleas!'
'Come along, Fido. We'd better not go in the house – she ——— it's full of fleas.'
3 Notice: 'Customers who consider our waitresses uncivil should see the manager.'
One could ——— from this notice that the manager is more uncivil than the waitresses.
4 Newspaper item: 'After tea, the Vicar presented the traditional gifts of money to the ten widows left by the late Captain Smith.'
If I did not happen to have known the Captain, I would say it ——— he was a much-married man.

LAY IS A TRANSITIVE VERB

I *lay* the table. I lay what?
I *lay* the table.
Table is the object of the transitive verb.
He *lays* the table; we *laid* the table; and they have *laid* the table.

LIE IS AN INTRANSITIVE VERB

I *lie* on the couch. I lie what?
I don't lie anything.
There is no object. *Lie* is an intransitive verb.
She *lies*; they *lay*; and you have *lain* on the couch.

For details of 'transitive' and 'intransitive' verbs, refer to page 25.

(a) Write out the following, putting *lay, lays, laid;* or *lie, lies, lain* in the blank spaces.

1 'Waiter, what's wrong with these eggs?' 'Don't ask me, sir, I only ——— the table.'
2 It's nice to get up in the morning but it's nicer to ——— in bed.
3 The fox now ——— asleep, dreaming of the chicken-house.
4 The stone that has ——— in one place becomes covered with moss.
5 A psychiatrist bought his little daughter a big doll. She doesn't play with it or ——— down with it; she ——— it on the couch and asks it questions.
6 'Lay down, pup,' ordered the postman. 'Good dog, lay down.' 'You'll have to say "——— down", mister,' said the small boy. 'That dog belongs to my English teacher.'

Laying is the present participle of the verb lay. It must have an object (it must be laying *something*). The verb in the drawing is *laying* – laying what? – *laying* a wall of bricks.

Lying is the present participle of the verb lie. It does *not* have an object (it is not possible to be lying *something*). The verb in the drawing is *lying* on top of the word 'lying.'

For details of the present participle refer to pages 30 and 31.

(a) Write out the following, putting *laying* or *lying* in the spaces.

1 The stone that has been ——— in one place becomes covered with moss.
2 'Waiter, what's wrong with these eggs?' 'Don't ask me, sir, all I do here is go round ——— the tables.'
3 It's nice to get up in the morning but it's nicer to be left ——— in bed.
4 The teacher was helping little Mary with her arithmetic problems. 'Imagine that I am ——— four eggs here and ——— five eggs over there, how many will I have?' Mary, ——— her pen down, slowly shook her head and said, 'I don't believe you can do it.'
5 The fox now ——— asleep is dreaming of the chicken-house.
6 'You see,' said the small boy, 'the dog is ——— down now. You only have to say the right word.'

RISE & RAISE

Raise your right hand and repeat...

RAISE IS A TRANSITIVE VERB
RISE IS INTRANSITIVE

Example of *raise:*
To understand your parents' love you must *raise* children yourself.
(Raise what? Raise children, the object of the transitive verb.)

Example of rise:
He that lies down with dogs shall *rise* up with fleas.
(Rise what? Just rise. There is no object with an intransitive verb.)

(a) Write out the following, putting *raise* and *rise* in the spaces.

1 Court Usher: 'Silence in court. The court will ———.'
2 Those motorists in favour of saving petrol, ——— your right foot.
3 'My little brother fell over the cliff. What shall I do?'
'Run to the library and get a book out on how to ——— a child.'
4 A conceited man is like the cockerel who thinks the sun has decided to ——— to hear him crow.
5 'I ——— to ——— the question of a new rose this season. As you all know, it is very expensive to ——— a new rose because costs always ——— at this time of year. But if we ——— ours first, our profits will ———.'

AFFECT & EFFECT

AFFECT IS THE ACTION
EFFECT IS THE RESULT

Affect is a verb, meaning 'to cause a change in something'.

Example:
Steroid drugs are banned because they *affect* an athlete's performance (cause a change in it).

Effect is a noun, meaning 'result or consequence'.

Example:
He promised to follow the rules, or words to that *effect* (having that result or consequence).

Effect is sometimes used as a verb, meaning 'to bring something into being'.

Example:
The doctor is using a new drug which he is sure will *effect* a complete cure for the disease (bring cure into being).

(a) Write out the following, putting *affect* or *effect* in the spaces.

1 Last night's rain had no ——— on the wicket. It could not ——— it because it was covered with sheets.
2 My sister can keep a secret with a 'telling' ———.
3 Repartee is perfect, when it can ——— its purpose with a double edge.
4 Words differently arranged ——— a different meaning, and meanings differently arranged have a different ———.

**Shall and will are auxiliary verbs (words that help to form the tenses of other verbs).
They form the future tense.**

1 *Shall* and *will* are used in two possible ways. The first way is to indicate simply that something will happen in the future, without anyone making a special effort to bring it about.

Example:
I shall:
I just love sunshine; when I go on holiday, *I shall* sit in the sun day and night.

We shall:
Live for today! In a hundred years time *we shall* all be bald.

He will and *she will:*
'Nurse, I'm at death's door!'
'Don't worry – the doctor says *he will* pull you through.'

You will:
Nervous lady to pilot: '*You will* bring me down safely, won't you?'
'Don't worry, lady, I've never left anybody up there yet.'

They will:
'What's going to become of the children?' wail the parents. Oh, *they will* grow old and worry about what will become of their children.

'I SHALL
just sit here quietly and read my newspaper.'

The man above is not showing any determination or effort in his future activity – it is just going to happen.

In cases like this, use *shall* with 'I' and 'we'; use *will* with 'you', 'he', 'she', 'it' and 'they'.

2 The second way to use *shall* and *will* is to indicate a command, a promise, or an expression of determination (*something is definitely going to happen*).

In order to show determination, you reverse all the simple rules: *shall* becomes *will*, and *will* becomes *shall*.

I will:
I am better than George Washington.
He said he could not tell a lie.
I *can* tell a lie but *I will* not.

We will:
'Why are you searching the beach?'
'For a piece of toffee!' said her husband.
'Don't let's waste time doing that.'
'*We will* have to,' he said, 'my false teeth are stuck to it.'

He shall and *she shall:*
I have decided to drown myself, and nobody *shall* save me.

You shall:
The mother says to her child:
'*You shall*!' and if the child is good, it says:
'I will.'

They shall:
There are no times like the old times – *they shall* never be allowed to fade from our memories.

'I WILL
have to take the dog out for a walk.'

The man above has declared his determination to perform a future activity – he is going to *make* something happen.

In cases like this, use *will* with 'I' and 'we'; use *shall* with 'you','he', 'she', 'it' and 'they'.

"Do you swear that the evidence you will give shall be the truth, the whole truth, and nothing but the truth?'

In this common form of wording in court, the witness is about to speak (it will simply happen) so he *will* give evidence. However, he is also asked to swear that he will speak only the truth (make a determined promise) so he is asked that the evidence *shall* be only the truth. This is therefore a mixture of the two rules.

(a) Write out the following, putting *shall* or *will* in the blank spaces. In some cases, you may feel either is possible, but give your reasons.

1 'Waiter, ——— I have to sit here until I starve to death?'
'No, sir – we close at eleven.'
2 Two fleas came out of the cinema. One said to the other, 'I say, ——— we walk, or take a dog?'
3 '——— you love me when I am old and ugly?'
'But darling, of course I do.'
4 Always bear in mind that if anything can go wrong, it ———.
5 Don't say, 'I ——— study when I find the time.' You may never find the time.
6 What the heart has once owned, it ——— never lose.
7 An inch of gold ——— not buy an inch of time.
8 If we are true to our past, we ——— not have to fear our future.
9 'I am the Genie of the Lamp; I ——— do whatever you wish.'
10 'I want a quarter-pound of rat poison.'
'Yes, sir, ——— I wrap it up, or ——— you eat it here?'
11 '——— you take this man to be your lawful wedded husband?'
'Er . . . um . . . well . . . oh, all right then: yes, I ———.'
12 'I swear that the evidence I ——— give ——— be the truth, the whole truth, and nothing but the truth.'
13 The lion and the lamb ——— lie down together but the lamb ——— not get much sleep!
14 Your old men ——— dream dreams; your young men ——— see visions.
15 Speak when you are angry, and you ——— make the best speech you ——— ever regret.
16 'This day is called the feast of Crispian:
He that outlives this day and comes safe home,
——— stand a tip-toe when this day is named,
And rouse him at the name of Crispian.
He that ——— live this day, and see old age,
——— yearly on the vigil feast his neighbours,
And say, 'These wounds I had on Crispian's day.'
Old men forget: yet all ——— be forgot.'
17 They ——— grow not old, as we that are left grow old:
Age ——— not weary them, nor the years condemn.
At the going down of the sun and in the morning
We ——— remember them.

Note: When using the conditional tense, *shall* becomes *should* and *will* becomes *would*.
For example:
'I *should* be grateful, and so *would* he, for any help.'

**A sentence has two parts:
the person or thing which the sentence is about, called *the subject*;
what is said or written about the subject, called *the predicate*.**

For example, look at this sentence describing the picture above:
The man asked the fortune-teller to tell him his future.

The *subject* is 'The man'.
The *predicate* is all the rest of the sentence, 'asked the fortune-teller to tell him his future'.

1 The predicate includes the verb of the sentence.

2 Sometimes the subject consists of a long group of words, for example:

Subject: The young man, pale from much worrying and many sleepless nights,
Predicate: asked about his future.

Who asked? 'The young man, pale from much worrying and many sleepless nights,' did the asking and is *the subject*.

3 Occasionally, in certain kinds of sentence, the subject is understood without actually being spoken or written, for example:
'Leave my house, and never return!'

Who has to leave? The subject 'you'.
'(You) leave my house, and never return!'

To begin every sentence with the subject would lead to monotony, and to avoid this we sometimes put the subject in the middle or at the end of a sentence, for example:
A dewdrop sparkled here and there.
Here and there *a dewdrop* sparkled.
Here and there sparkled *a dewdrop.*

(a) Write out the following, supplying suitable subjects to the predicates.

1 ——— was torn from the book.
2 ——— were torn from the book.
3 ——— saw Mary two weeks ago.
4 Two weeks ago ——— saw Mary.
5 Every year ——— both go camping.
6 At the end of the street lives ———.
7 ——— all grow in her front garden.
8 They ran to the edge and into the swimming pool dived ———.
9 On the stands at the furniture exhibition were displayed ———.
10 ——— is having his palm read by the famous Madame Predicate.

(b) Write out the following, supplying suitable predicates to the subjects.

1 Madame Predicate ———
2 My next-door neighbour ———
3 The tall trees on the hill ———
4 The magician and the jester ———
5 ——— the brave soldiers.
6 ——— a crash of thunder.
7 ——— a wounded tiger ———.
8 ——— the radiant bride ———.
9 My excuse ———.
10 ——— a school holiday.

A simple sentence has only one subject and one predicate.

Example:
The girl (subject) *opened the window* (predicate).

The same sentence could take the form of a question:
Did the girl open the window?

It could also take the form of a spoken order:
'Open the window!'
(the subject '*you*' has been left out because it is 'understood')

In the above drawings, the single rower represents the *simple sentence* and the pair of rowers represent the *compound sentence.* It is important to note the the single rower has *just one oar* to make his boat move, because the simple sentence has *just one verb.* The pair of rowers each have an oar, because the compound sentence (consisting of two or more simple sentences) must have *more than one verb.*

In the following sentences, note the *single verb* in each one.

The lion *crouched.* It *gave* a fierce growl. It *was* about to attack. The hunter *dropped* to one knee. He *raised* the gun to his shoulder.

The simple sentence should not be used all the 'me, because longer sentences will provide ›ore variety.

A compound sentence is made up of two or more simple sentences joined by a conjunction or separated by a semi-colon.

Example:
She *entered* the room. (one verb)
She *did not sit* down. (one verb)
She entered the room *but* she did not sit down. (two verbs)

Never *envy* a rich man. (one verb)
He *is* only a poor man with money. (one verb)
Never envy a rich man; he is only a poor man with money. (two verbs)

Note that the separate parts of the compound sentence still make complete sense if you take away the conjunction or semi-colon.

(a) Write out the following, forming compound sentences from the pairs of simple sentences.

1 The girls work hard.
The boys are lazy.
2 Shall I make a telephone-call?
Will you write a letter to him?
3 The audience burst into applause.
The hall echoed with the clapping.
4 They came home exhausted.
They had been on a marathon run.
5 Carnivorous animals are predators.
Herbivorous animals feed on plants.

SUBJECT AND OBJECT

SIR ISAAC NEWTON (SUBJECT) OBSERVED THE APPLE (OBJECT)

The object in a sentence is the person or thing to whom the action of the verb is done.

Look back to page 25.

1 To find the object of a sentence, ask 'whom' or 'what' *after* the verb.

Examples:
The Headteacher *presented* the prizes.
The Headteacher presented 'what'?
Answer: the prizes (object)

The Headteacher *praised* the head-girl.
The Headteacher praised 'whom'?
Answer: the head-girl (object)

The object is enclosed within the predicate part of the sentence (see page 42). The predicates of the above examples are:
'presented the prizes' and 'praised the head-girl'.

2 Sometimes the object takes the form of a group of words, for example:

I *heard* that you came top of the class.
I heard 'what'?
Answer: that you came top of the class (object)

3 There is another kind of 'object' called the *indirect object.*

Example:
The Headteacher *presented* the prize to the head-girl.
The Headteacher presented 'what'?
Answer: the prize (object)
The prize was presented 'to whom'?
Answer: the head-girl (indirect object)

The Headteacher *gave* her the prize.
The Headteacher gave 'what'?
Answer: the prize (object)
He gave it 'to whom'?
Answer: to her (indirect object)
The *indirect object* is introduced by 'to' or 'for'.

In this second example, the 'to' is not stated, but it is understood.

4 A sentence which has a *being* word for a verb (for example, *is, are, was, were*) never has an object.

Examples:
That girl *is* my best friend.
('*That girl*' and '*my best friend*' are one and the same person.)

5 Sometimes it is necessary to repeat the object, or refer to it with a pronoun, to avoid ambiguity.

Example:
Club Notice: Will members kindly empty tea-pots, rinse round, and, before leaving, please stand upside down in the sink?

Correction:
Club Notice: Will members kindly empty tea-pots, rinse round, and, before leaving, please stand *the tea-pots* (or please stand *them*) upside down in the sink?

SUBJECT & OBJECT PRONOUNS

Certain pronouns are used when they are *the subject* of a sentence, and others are used when they are *the object* of a sentence.

The *subject* pronouns are:
I he she we they

The *object* pronouns are:
me him her us them

Note: The pronouns *it* and *you* are used for both subject and object.

There may be times when you are uncertain whether to use the subject or object pronoun, for example, should you write:
'John is much stronger than *I*.'
or should it be:
'John is much stronger than *me*.'

You can test which one to use by 'extending' the sentence, as follows:
John is much stronger than *I* am strong.
The subject pronoun *I* must be correct, because you obviously could not write:
'than *me* am strong.'

Again, should you write:
'Janet and *she* are going to the park.'
or should it be:
'Janet and *her* are going to the park.'?

Janet is going to the park and *she* is going to the park.
The subject pronoun *she* must be correct.

(a) Write out the following, putting the correct pronouns in the blank spaces. Then say whether each is the subject or object of the sentence.

1 'Will you join Janet and ———?'
'Why, are you two coming apart?'
2 Friends are people who dislike the same people as ——— do.
3 'I wouldn't like to do the work John does.'
'I agree; rather ——— than ———.'
4 The boys at our table ate so much, we had less to eat than ———.
5 When my sister and ——— told the doctor about our loss of memory, he made ——— and ——— pay in advance,

After prepositions, we always use the *object* pronouns (refer to page 28).

For example:
'The secret is between you and *me*.'
Why not 'between you and *I*'?
Because *between* is a preposition.

(b) Write out the following, putting the correct pronouns in the blank spaces.

1 She gave the parcel to my brother and ———.
2 'Share this with your brother; I made it specially for you and ———.'
3 I saw Jane in the front row and sat down beside ———.

Note: For the correct use of the pronouns *who* and *whom*, refer to Book 1, page 55.

THE PHRASE

A phrase is group of words without a verb, which is therefore not a complete sentence.

Example:
in its mother's pouch
(This does not make sense on its own.)

Add a subject to the phrase:
the baby kangaroo

Add a verb to the phrase:
lives

The result is a complete sentence:
The baby kangaroo lives *in its mother's pouch.*

In the drawing, *the sentence* is shown as a mother kangaroo and *the phrase* as a baby. A baby kangaroo cannot exist outside its mother's pouch; in the same way, a phrase cannot 'exist' outside the sentence.

(a) Turn the following phrases into sentences by adding words which must include a verb.

Example:
Before going to sleep ———
Before going to sleep, I set my alarm for seven o'clock.

1 A few days ago ———
2 At the end of the street ———
3 ——— during the holidays.
4 ——— a horse without a rider.
5 ——— like a greyhound ———
6 ——— carrying a cargo of machinery ———

A phrase may be used to take the place of an adjective, an adverb or a noun, making it possible to write longer and more interesting sentences.

Examples of the *adjectival phrase* taking the place of the adjective:

The *tired* mountaineer rested for a while on a flat ledge.
The mountaineer, *tired with his long and strenuous climb,* rested for a while on a flat ledge.
His *lined* face showed clear signs of the strain of the climb.
His face, *lined with exhaustion and lack of sleep,* showed clear signs of the strain of the climb.

Examples of the *adverb phrase* taking the place of the adverb:

She asked her teacher if she could sit *there.*
She asked her teacher if she could sit *at the desk in the corner of the class-room.*

The tiger *silently* stalked the zebra.
Without making the slightest sound, the tiger stalked the zebra.

Example of the *noun phrase* taking the place of the noun:

His *residence* has a fine view.
His *detached bungalow with scarlet shutters* has a fine view.

Example of the *noun phrase* giving more information about the noun, but not replacing it:

The school journey last year was to *Lisbon.*
The school journey last year was to *the historic city of Lisbon, capital of Portugal.*

(b) There is a phrase, 'straight from the horse's mouth'. As horses don't actually talk, explain the meaning of this phrase and guess how it may have originated.

THE CLAUSE

A clause is a subdivision of a sentence which includes a verb.

Example of a clause with its verb:
unless you work hard

This clause doesn't make sense on its own, but if you add another clause you can make a complete sentence, for example:
You cannot succeed *unless you work hard.*

In the drawing at the top, the clauses are represented as a set of 'Russian dolls': when they are fitted together, they make a complete whole.

1 Clauses are divided into different kinds according to the job they do in the sentence. The most important clause is *the main clause,* and it can stand by itself and make complete sense. It is the only clause that is able to be independent of the rest of the sentence.

2 The other clauses are various kinds of *subordinate clauses.* A person who is a subordinate works under the control of another person. The subordinate clause works under the control of the main clause.

In order to make sense, a sentence should have a main clause (sometimes more than one) and as many subordinate clauses as are required.

Example of a main clause:
I ran all the way to school.
(this makes complete sense by itself)

You may add a subordinate clause:
because I was very late
(this does not make sense by itself, but it adds an explanation.)

put the two clauses together:
I ran all the way to school because I was very late.

The main clause does not have to go first. You could also say:
Because I was very late, I ran all the way to school.

(a) The following *main* and *subordinate* clause have been separated.
Combine each main clause with an appropriate subordinate and underline the *main clause.*

Example:
The house is a large one
which stands at the corner
The house, which stands at the corner, is a large one.

A film is showing at the cinema
that I think will interest you
A film that I think will interest you is showing at the cinema.

1 he did not know the day
2 which has the world's largest oil reserves
3 let me know
4 who had long blonde hair
5 Saudi-Arabia is a country
6 where new records are sold cheaply
7 unless you work very hard
8 which had been attacking hard for most of the game
9 I know a department-store
10 the girl won the beauty contest
11 you will not pass the examination
12 when the results would be announced
13 the team scored the winning goal in the final minute
14 when you have made up your mind

The complex sentence consists of a main clause with one (or more than one) subordinate clause, with a verb in each.

Example:
After the girl had written the address on the envelope, she posted the letter.

The main clause:
She posted (verb) the letter.
(It makes sense on its own.)

The subordinate clause:
After the girl had written (verb) the address on the envelope
(It has a verb, but can only exist within a longer sentence.)

The subordinate clause may be at the beginning or the end of the sentence, or (as in the following example) fitted inside the main clause:

The main clause:
The fox has been caught.
The subordinate clause:
that killed the chickens
The complex sentence:
The fox that killed the chickens has been caught.

To be 'subordinate' means to be of inferior importance or rank. In the drawing at the top, the *subordinate clauses* are shown as private soldiers taking orders from the sergeant (above them in rank) who is shown as the *main clause.*

The following gives some idea of the flexibility of the complex sentence.

Simple sentence (the main clause):
The little boy refused to go to bed.
Add a subordinate adverb clause:
because he was obstinate
Add another subordinate adverb clause:
when his mother reasoned with him

The sentence can now be written in any of the following patterns:

When his mother reasoned with him, the little boy refused to go to bed, because he was obstinate.

The little boy refused to go to bed when his mother reasoned with him, because he was obstinate.

Because he was obstinate, the little boy refused to go to bed when his mother reasoned with him.

The little boy, because he was obstinate, refused to go to bed when his mother reasoned with him.

(a) Here is another complex sentence:

Simple sentence (the main clause):
The audience burst into applause.
One subordinate clause added:
calling for an encore
Second subordinate clause added:
as the orchestra finished

Write out the above sentence in as many patterns as you can think of.

1 A *simple sentence* contains only one subject and one predicate (see page 43).

2 A *compound sentence* consists of two or more simple sentences joined by a conjunction (see page 43).

The test of a compound sentence is that when you separate the clauses, each will still make complete sense.

An example of a compound sentence made from two simple sentences:
Elizabeth went out shopping.
Janet helped with the dishes.
Elizabeth went out shopping *and* Janet helped with the dishes.

A compound sentence may also be formed by using a *semi-colon* or a *colon* (see pages 6 and 8).

There may be any number of clauses in a compound sentence, provided each is completely independent. For example:

Elizabeth went out shopping.
Janet helped with the dishes.
John sat watching television.
Elizabeth went out shopping *and* Janet helped with the dishes, *but* John sat watching television.

A famous pianist was booked to play at the prison last week. The concert was cancelled. Someone stole the piano.
A famous pianist was booked to play at the prison last week, *but* the concert was cancelled *because* someone stole the piano.

3 A *complex sentence* contains one main clause and one or more subordinate *(dependent)* clauses. Unlike the clauses of a compound sentence, they are not of equal importance; only the main clause can stand alone without relying on another clause.

Examples of how to form complex sentences:

The pond was safe for skating.
It had frozen during the night.
The pond, *which had frozen during the night*, was safe for skating.

A cannibal went to see a psychiatrist.
He was fed up with people.
A cannibal *who was fed up with people* went to see a psychiatrist.

We call our goalkeeper 'Cinderella'.
He keeps missing the ball.
We call our goalkeeper 'Cinderella' *because he keeps missing the ball.*

Note that one of the simple sentences each time has become a subordinate clause (in italics) which no longer makes complete sense on its own.

4 A *compound–complex sentence* has more than one main clause plus one or more subordinate clauses.

Example:
The audience burst into applause.
(first main clause)
The hall echoed with the clapping.
(second main clause)
As the orchestra finished
(subordinate clause)
As the orchestra finished, the audience burst into applause, and the hall echoed with the clapping.

5 A useful way of joining two sentences into one simple sentence is by changing one of the verbs into a *present participle* (see pages 30 and 32) and omitting the unwanted pronoun.

Example:
At the brewery, a man *fell* into a tank of beer.
He came to a bitter end.
At the brewery, a man *falling* into a tank of beer came to a bitter end.

Mary enjoyed her holiday in Rome.
She managed to pick up a little Italian.
Mary enjoyed her holiday in Rome, *managing* to pick up a little Italian.

'PULLED' AND 'PUSHED' SENTENCES

The 'pulled sentence' is one which starts with the main idea and is followed by one or more subordinate ideas.

The 'pushed sentence' is one in which the main idea is held in suspense until near the end of the sentence.

The great majority of sentences are written in the 'pulled' style. The 'pushed sentence' is used for special emphasis.

A 'pulled sentence':
The true test of civilization is not the census, nor the size of cities, nor the crops, but the kind of person that the country turns out.

A 'pushed sentence':
It is not the census, nor the size of cities, nor the crops, but the kind of person that the country turns out that is *the true test of civilization.*

A 'pulled sentence':
The greatest pleasure I know is to do a good action by stealth and have it found out by accident.

A 'pushed sentence':
To do a good action by stealth and have it found out by accident is *the greatest pleasure I know.*

What is the effect on the reader of a 'pushed sentence' compared with a 'pulled sentence'?

(a) Write out the following sentences in the 'pushed sentence' style.

1 *Parents would appreciate their children more* if they stopped to realize that the film of childhood can never have a second showing.
2 *Entertaining would be a lot easier* if you could just convince yourself that guests don't expect any more at your house than you do at theirs.
3 *Where there is no love,* a crowd is not company, faces are but a gallery of pictures, and talk but a tinkling cymbal.

(b) Write out the following sentences in the 'pulled sentence' style.

1 The pursuit of the uneatable by the unspeakable is the sport of fox hunting.
2 The record of mankind in quest of daily bread is the history of the world.
3 The capacity to see our faults is perhaps the only true dignity we have.
4 Had it happened to be within the reach of greedy human hands, the moon would have disappeared long ago.
5 Even though the world may write them down as failures, the people who have done their level best, and who know that they have done their best, are a success.

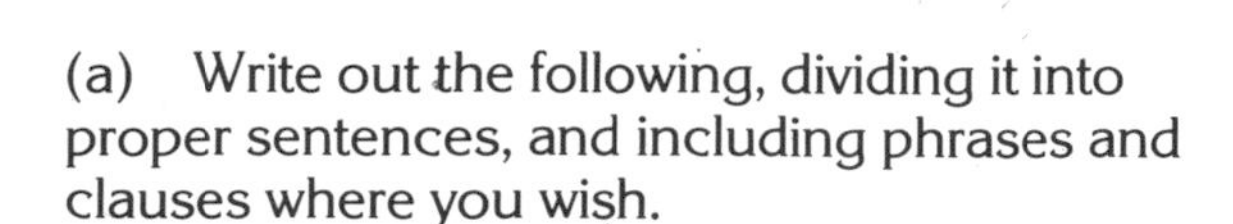

SENTENCE EXERCISES

(a) Write out the following, dividing it into proper sentences, and including phrases and clauses where you wish.

Department-store notice

There is a very good reason for this notice being here and you standing in front of it reading it it is here to keep you busy we realize how annoying it can be just standing round doing nothing trying to find someone to help you consequently we have this notice here for you to read, and hope that by the time you finish reading it one of our staff will have found you if not, would you please read this notice again.

(b) The following story has been divided into simple sentences . Write them out in as few sentences as good style will allow, using compound and complex sentences. Remember that the occasional simple sentence can be used effectively. For example:

My memory is remarkably good. There are only three things I can't remember. I can't remember faces. I can't remember names. I have forgotten the third thing.

My memory is so remarkably good that there are only three things I can't remember: faces, names and . . . I have forgotten the third thing.

1 John Smith desperately wanted to be a great actor. He went to an audition for the part of Abraham Lincoln in a new play. He dressed up to look exactly like the great man. He wore a top-hat, a red sash, a black frockcoat and big shiny boots. On his head he wore a black curly wig. He made his face up to look like Lincoln. He put on a large false nose and a fringe beard. He learnt by heart the Gettysburg Address. Abraham Lincoln had made this speech after the decisive battle of Gettysburg. He did not get the part. On his way home, he was assassinated.

(c) The Editor of a small local newspaper dismissed his reporter because his news items were so badly written. If you can rewrite the following to the Editor's satisfaction, you may get the reporter's job.

1 INCIDENT AT WEDDING RECEPTION
It was just after the assembled guests had toasted the bride that her wedding gown started to go brown and smoulder, but fortunately it was soon put out.

2 SOLDIER TO BE PUT ON A CHARGE
A soldier has been accused of setting fire to his blankets while smoking in bed and the hut had to be evacuated. After the fire had been extinguished, the accused got into a spare sleeping-bag, followed by the other seventeen occupants of the hut.

3 VALUABLE ADVICE FROM VILLAGE VET
A dog has been discovered suffering from distemper and I would advise anyone who has a dog to be inoculated. Bottles of dog-tonic should be kept in a safe place, and if there are children in the house, lock them in a small metal box.

4 VACANCY AT THE COUNCIL OFFICE
Any school-leaver who wishes to apply should give the names, addresses and professions of two referees. They should not be your school-teachers, but responsible persons of mature age who are well acquainted with you.

THE SIMILE
'Get your hair cut! You look like a chrysanthemum!'

SIMILES COMPARE

ONE THING WITH ANOTHER

A simile is a figure of speech in which a comparison is made between two things and one is said to be *like* another.

The most common words to introduce a simile are the following:

as, like, as if, as though, as (something) as, much the same as, seems, resembles, is similar to, in the image of, in the manner of.

Example:
That silly boy behaves *like* a donkey.
as if he was a donkey
in the manner of, etc.

The simile is frequently used in poetry, but even in prose – if it is used imaginatively – the simile can add style to your work.

The similes we often use in speech, such as 'as cunning as a fox', 'like water off a duck's back', and so on, are acceptable for daily usage, but are often too familiar and 'worn out' for use in written work.

Similes may be short and concise for a simple comparison, or extended to suit the expression of a detailed image or pattern of thought.

Examples:
The seagulls spread their wings *like arched eyebrows.*

The road lay curling around the fields, *the image of a ribbon lost from the dress of a careless summer.*

Here are some more examples of the common introduction in use:

She is *as* beautiful *as* a flower in a seed catalogue.

He had a face that looked *as though* it had worn out four bodies.

The feeling of friendship *is similar to* being comfortably filled with roast beef.

They wandered about at random, *in the manner of* dogs that have lost the scent.

(a) Write out the following ten similes, using your imagination to put suitable words in the spaces.

1. The boxer had a hand resembling a bunch of ———.
2. His face looked like ——— that had refused to set and was about to run.
3. He is as ——— as a dinosaur.
4. When she smiled after frowning, it was as if the ——— was coming out from behind the ———.
5. A snowflake is rather like a ——— wearing a white fur coat.
6. Those two are about as ——— as a cat and a goldfish.
7. Telling a lie is like ———: the wound may heal, but the scar will remain.
8. I heard a multitude of tongues, like the whispering ——— of tall ——— stirred by the wind.
9. Our country has changed. Once we roared like ——— for liberty; now we bleat like ——— for security.
10. The mind of a bigoted person resembles the ——— of an ———; the more light yc pour upon it, the more it will contract.

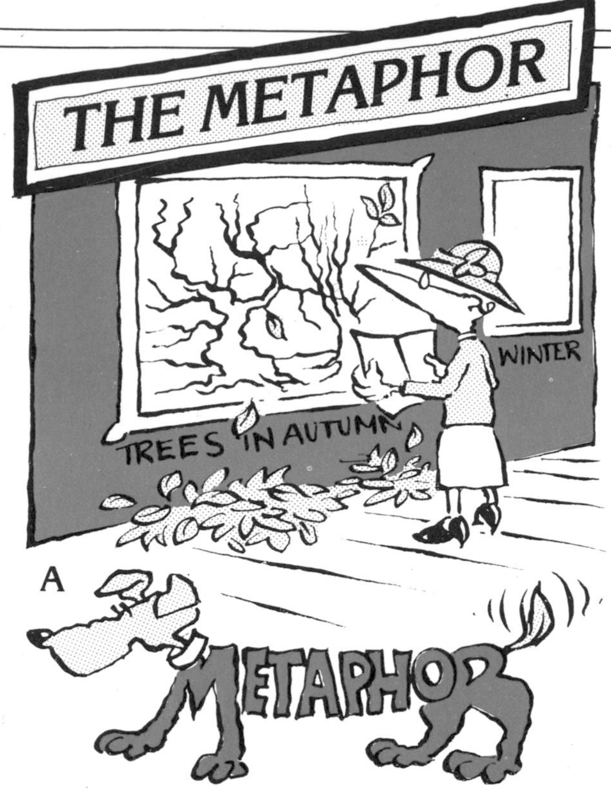

PRETENDS IT IS SOMETHING ELSE

A metaphor is a figure of speech in which a comparison is made by saying that one thing *is* something else.

A metaphor can be a single word or a group of words, for example:

Boiling with anger, she *snapped my head off* when I became impertinent.

A person cannot 'boil' and nobody was actually decapitated, but the sentence is more lively and vivid than it would be without the metaphors.

The metaphor does not use the introductory 'as' or 'like' of the simile, but simply describes one thing in terms of another. There are three qualities to be noted in good metaphorical language, and these are:

The picture or image suggested should be lear and realistic enough to be easily sualized.

e metaphor should be concisely expressed maximum impact.

The impression will be stronger if it is novel: metaphors which are stale through over-use no longer conjure up the original image.

The metaphor is used far more often than the simile both in speech and in writing. Without being aware of it, we speak in metaphors when we describe a person as '*dead* lazy' or something as '*dirt* cheap'. We refer to '*skyscrapers*', 'traffic *bottlenecks*' and '*watertight* security'.

Newspapers make frequent use of the metaphor. They might announce that 'The Minister *came under fire* in the Commons today', without meaning that he was actually being shot at. In the sporting pages one might read, 'Smith *grows in stature* with every match he plays.' Look through your newspaper and write out what you consider to be good metaphors – and bad ones.

(a) In your own words, explain fully the meanings of the following:

1 A black cat dropped soundlessly from a high wall, a spoonful of dark treacle which melted under the gate.
2 An actor is a sculptor who carves in snow.
3 Great architecture is frozen music.
4 A good painting is a poem without words.
5 Poetry is an attempt to paint the colour of the wind.
6 Words are nails for fixing ideas.
7 A child is not a bowl to be filled, but a fire to be lit.
8 A best-selling novel is often a deluge of words and a drizzle of thoughts.

(b) Write down what you think the metaphors in this verse stand for.

Awake! for morning in the bowl of night
Has flung the stone that puts the stars to flight.
And lo! The Hunter of the East has caught
The Sultan's turret in a noose of light.

Young poet: 'Do you think I should put more *fire* in my poetry?'
Editor: 'No. I think you should put more of your poetry in the fire!'

Alliteration is the repeating of a letter to produce a particular effect.

Example:
*S*he *s*ells *s*ea-*sh*ells on the *s*ea-*sh*ore.
(a 'tongue-twister')
The child is listening to the *s*oft *s*ound*s* of the *s*urging *s*ea e*s*caping from a *s*ea-*sh*ell found on the *sh*ore.
(the effect of the sea on the beach)

Some advertisers make use of the device in their jingles, to obtain a memorable or humorous effect, for example:
'Only *p*icked when the *p*eas go *p*o*p*!'

(a) In the following extract, similar use of alliteration has been used to obtain a different effect. Explain the effect the poet has tried to convey.

'The*s*e are dead face*s*.
*W*asp'*s* ne*s*ts are not *s*o *w*anly *w*axen,
*W*ood ember*s* not *s*o greyly ashen.'

Note that although the first letter of a word used as alliteration is the most important, letters in the middle or end of a word may also be used.

(b) Make up some sentences based on scenes from nature, with one letter predominating in each.

Examples:
The *m*idsummer *m*eadows were *m*inting coins of *m*arigolds.

I hear *l*ake water *l*apping with *l*ow sounds by the shore.

Onomatopeia is the use of words which imitate or suggest the sound of what they describe

Examples:
Whisper has the 'hissing' sound of voices deliberately hushed.
Giggle imitates the high-pitched laughter of small children.
Screech creates the impression of a loud response to terror or pain.

The use of words with an effective sound-value can intensify your meaning.
Compare these two:
The witch gave a sinister *laugh.*
The witch gave a sinister *cackle.*

As well as imitating actual sound, onomatopeiac words may be used in a symbolic manner, for example:
The saw was *panting* through a plank.

Onomatopeia is principally used for poetry and is often a good accompaniment to alliteration, for example:

The *murmuring* of innumerable bees ...

Over the cobbles he *clattered* and *clashed* ...

Dim drums *throbbing* in the hills half heard ...

Strong gongs *groaning* as the guns boom far ...

Plangent, hidden from eyes, somewhere
An eukaleli *thrills* and cries ...

Now the hungry lion *roars,*
And the wolf be*howls* the moon ...

And the *hip-hop-hap* of the *clap* of the hands
And the *ting-tong-tang* of the guitar ...

'I used to be a were-wolf, but I'm much bette
now-ooo-ow-ooo ...'

A synonym is a word that has almost the same meaning as another word.

(a) Write four sentences using one of the following synonyms in each sentence. Your sentences should make clear the slight difference in meaning of each of the four words.

big large huge immense

Example:
I feel quite *tired* after that long walk.
My aunt was *fatigued* after the excitement of her eightieth birthday.

Fatigued is a synonym for *tired:*
it means almost the same.

In the drawing above, the 'film-star' rests while his 'stand-in' (who must be very like him) takes his place. Similarly, the synonym must be very like the word it replaces. In addition, it must always be the same part of speech; the synonym for an adjective must itself be an adjective, and so on.

(b) Write out synonyms for the following. If you are not sure of the meaning of any of them, check in a dictionary.

comprehend	completely	calamity
investigation	project	reasonable
student	graphic	intelligence
colossal	antiquated	modest
construct	obstructing	hobby
ecreation	trustworthy	predict
place	hazardous	friend
assin	plenty	sympathetic
session	paternal	

An antonym is a word with a meaning opposite to another word.

Examples:
harmony: its antonym is discord
discord: its antonym is harmony

1 The antonym must also be the same part of speech as its partner, for example:

angel: its antonym is devil (nouns)
angelic: its antonym is devilish (adjectives)

2 Sometimes there are several antonyms you could choose, so that you can select a word with the precise shade of meaning you require, for example:

slow: fast, speedy, quick, rapid, hasty.

3 Many antonyms may be formed by the addition of a prefix (giving the negative form), such as:

dis-, in-, mis-, un-, non-

Examples:
necessary: *un*necessary
luminous: *non*-luminous
satisfied: *dis*satisfied

4 Words ending in the suffix *-ful* can form their opposites by replacing the *-ful* with the suffix *-less*, for example:
harm*ful*: harm*less*

(a) Write out antonyms for the following:

shallow	admitted	modern
compulsory	encourage	interior
knowledge	spendthrift	optimist
allowed	frequently	expanding

REDUNDANCY

Redundancy is the use of superfluous words or phrases, when their meaning is already clear from other words or phrases.

Example:
I must decline to accept your kind offer.

The word 'decline' politely implies that one cannot accept, making the words 'to accept' redundant. There are two possible ways to rewrite this sentence.

I must decline your kind offer.
I regret that I am unable to accept your kind offer.

The winner of the beauty contest will fly to Paris, with all expenses paid, and will stay two nights in a luxury hotel without needing to spend a penny.

The sentence should be rewritten as:

The winner of the beauty contest will fly to Paris, with all expenses paid, and will stay two nights in a luxury hotel.

(a) Rewrite the following sentence avoiding all the redundant phrases.

The Judge dismissed two members of the jury, because he had reason to believe that one sixth of the jury had already made up their minds on the verdict and in view of their bias could not be relied upon to base their verdict on the evidence.

Note: Redundant phrases should be given 'dismissal notices' because a good sentence cannot afford to carry words which have no useful work to do.

TAUTOLOGY

'Let's divide it into two equal halves.'

Tautology is the use of an extra word or phrase which pointlessly repeats an idea in the sentence.

Examples:
The two girls, who are both alike, both agree with each other completely.

If two girls are alike, there is no need for the word 'both'; if two girls agree, it is obvious they *both* agree.
The sentence should be rewritten as:

The two girls, who are alike, agree with each other completely.

The annual insurance premium due is to be paid every year.

'Annual' is the same as 'every year'.
'A premium due' is a premium which has to be paid.
The sentence should be rewritten as:

The insurance premium is to be paid every year.

(a) Rewrite the following, leaving out any words you consider tautological.

1 'I'm not sure whether to cut this cake into two equal halves or into four quarters.'
2 The soldier died from fatal wounds.
3 'Please repeat that question again.'
4 'It is just exactly four o'clock.'
5 The plan is nearing final completion.
6 'She is equally as clever as me.'
7 'Assemble together in the hall!'
8 'Notice how I have not omitted any important essentials in the scheme I have introduced as a new innovation.'

Verbosity is the use of too many words or too long words, where brevity would be more effective.

Good plain language should be *clear, simple* and *concise.* It is sometimes essential to use long words, but only if short, simple words cannot produce the desired effect. Never use more words in a sentence than are necessary to express the meaning. In particular, be careful to avoid *redundancy* and *tautology.*

To achieve conciseness in writing, ensure that all words are carrying their proper load of meaning and helping other words to do the same. There is, however, a difference between *brevity* for its own sake and *conciseness.* Do not cut out words simply for the sake of being brief, or you might lose some good qualities, such as variety, imagination and – above all – accuracy.

The following are some examples of verbosity to be avoided:

'due to the fact that' for 'because'
'I am of the opinion that' for 'I think'
'reach a decision' for 'decide'
'at this moment in time' for 'now'

Customer: 'Give me some prepared monaceticacidester of salicyclic acid.'
Chemist: 'Do you mean aspirin?'
Customer: 'That's right! I can never think of that name.'

(a) The following is a verbose (much exaggerated) version of a famous speech; compare it with the original.

'Companions, Citizens of the Eternal City, Compatriots, pay particular attention to the oration I am about to deliver.

At this moment in time I am addressing you in the capacity of funeral director of our deceased ruler rather than as that person's public relations adviser.

The memory of the oppressive nature of the actions performed by persons during their lifetime frequently survives their demise, but their more generous propensities tend all too often to be consigned to oblivion immediately following upon their decease.

In the case of our late lamented leader it is desirable that the customary practice should be adhered to.'

(b) Teacher: 'When Lot's wife looked back, what happened to her?'
Elizabeth (who has a very high IQ): 'Please miss, she was transmuted into a column of chloride of sodium.'

What would be a more simple answer?

(c) There is a well-known proverb which implies that undue multiplicity of personnel assigned either concurrently or consecutively to a single function involves deterioration in the resultant product as compared with the produce of an exact sufficiency of personnel.

How is this proverb usually written?

(d) 'What would you like with your fried eggs, dear?
'I would like some edible tubers fragmented and subsequently immersed in seething emollient fluid, transmogrified into brittle morsels of an amber shade of brown.'
'Very well, dear, but why can't you just say you want . . . . .?'

What did he want with his fried eggs?

A verbose writer never uses a sentence where a paragraph will do

Ambiguity occurs when there is more than one meaning to a sentence, and you cannot be certain which was intended.

The picture seems to show a man walking down a flight of steps with another man apparently floating in space; turn the picture upside-down and the 'floating' man is seen to be walking down the steps with the first man apparently 'floating'. The picture is ambiguous.

If your sentence is so awkwardly written that the meaning is confused, and the reader has to add his or her own interpretation to work out which meaning was intended, the sentence should be rewritten to remove the ambiguity. Ask yourself, what would I say if I were explaining this to somebody new? Then write it out in the closest style to your simple explanation.

1 There are four main ways in which ambiguity may arise, the commonest one being the incorrect position of a word, phrase, or clause; for example:

As in previous years, the evening ended with a toast to the new club president in champagne, provided by the retiring president, *drunk as usual at midnight*.

This should be re-written as:
As in previous years, the evening ended with a toast, *drunk as usual at midnight*, in champagne provided by the retiring president.

For ambiguities caused by the incorrect placing of the present participle, refer to page 32; for incorrect placing of the word 'only', see page 27.

2 The second most common form of ambiguity is the use of possessive adjectives or pronouns without making it quite clear to whom they refer, for example:

If the baby does not thrive on fresh milk *it* should be boiled.

Correction:
If the baby does not thrive on fresh milk, *the milk* should be boiled.

Elizabeth asked *her* sister when she wanted to listen to *her* new cassette.

Elizabeth asked *her* sister when she wanted to listen to *Elizabeth's* new cassette.

3 The third form is poor punctuation, and examples may be found on pages 1 and 2 (The hyphen) and page 11 (Correct placing of the comma).

4 The fourth form is the use of a word or words which have more than one meaning, for example:

Tommy: 'Will you do my homework for me?'
Father: 'No, it wouldn't be *right*.'
Tommy: 'Well, at least you could try.'
('right' can mean *morally proper* or it can mean *correct*)

(a) Rewrite the following sentences, removing all ambiguities.

1 'There's a man outside with a wooden leg named Smith.'
2 'I want you to keep that dog out of the house because it's full of fleas!'
3 The fire was put out before any damage could be done by the volunteer fire brigade.
4 'Roberts, the Furrier and Taxidermist. Customers' own skins dried and stuffed.'
5 It is reported that the vessel sank with all aboard except one lady passenger. She wa insured for a large sum and was heavily loaded with pig iron.

CLICHÉS

Clichés are expressions that have been used so often that they have lost their original effect.

Phrases which have now become clichés often began as interesting and distinctive expressions, but after being used over and over again, all their sparkle and originality have disappeared.

Avoid using the first stock phrase that comes to mind, and try to think of a fresh and personal way of using words. Your writing will be more original in style if you think of your own forms of expression.

Clichés can be put into six types:

1 Over-used adjectives, such as: the *acid* test; *tumultuous* applause; the *psychological* moment.

2 Stale figures of speech, such as: 'meek as a lamb'; 'cold as charity'; 'the staff of life.'

3 Over-worked quotations, such as: 'The lady doth protest too much'; 'Footprints on the sands of time'.

4 Worn-out foreign phrases, such as: *femme fatale; enfant terrible; blasé; sotto voce.*

5 Too-familiar idiomatic and proverbial expressions, such as: 'the writing on the wall'; 'take the bull by the horns'.

6 Repetitious fashionable phrases: 'wind of change'; 'the generation gap'; 'the inflationary spiral'; 'a "Catch 22" situation'.

(a) List the clichés in the following, and then rewrite the speech without using a single cliché!

'Ladies and Gentlemen of the Committee. As you know, I was given the unenviable task of speaking to the management.

I informed them that at this moment in time, they must descend from their ivory tower and look the facts squarely in the face. At the risk of making myself *persona non grata,* I pointed out that in this day and age, the rank and file have the right to prior consultation *à propos* the question of increased productivity. Although we believe in keeping a low profile, we are just as production-orientated and appreciative of difficult obstacles, economy-wise, as they themselves, I said.

At the end of the day, I told them, we must make a clean sweep of the problems arising at grass-roots level from the factory floor. In so many words, and not to put too fine a point on it, we had to fight tooth and nail to keep to the basic fundamentals in hopefully finding a mutual *terra firma* for industrial peace with all and sundry. On our side, we are fully prepared to give top priority to arriving at a harmonious settlement right across the board, with no strings attached.

We have no wish, I stated, to find ourselves looking back with hindsight, in an agonizing reappraisal, regretting that we let the grass grow under our feet, while all the time there was something rotten in the state of Denmark! We hoped our words would not fall on stony ground, but bearing in mind that he who hesitates is hopelessly lost, we are determined to explore every avenue and leave no stone unturned in order to have a full and meaningful discussion, getting down to the nitty-gritty without beating about the bush.

It was our intention that in making a blue-print for the future, we would put all we could into the pipeline, because that was the name of the game.

We appreciated that as captains of industry, they paid the piper and called the tune, but as of now, we wish to hold out the olive-branch of *pax,* because in the final analysis, without a common platform of agreement, their hopes would be blighted, and we would have a winter of discontent.'

GALLICISMS

Gallicisms are words and phrases borrowed from French.

The English language first began to borrow French words after the Norman Conquest, and the process has continued up to the present time, chiefly in the areas of the arts, fashion and cooking.

A large number of words have been in the language so long that they have been 'adopted' and are now considered as English words, for example:

ballet	blancmange	bureau
colonel	connoisseur	coupon
café	chauffeur	debris
depot	fiancé	gateau
lingerie	matinée	menu
meringue	petite	trousseau

This is a continuing process.

'Adopted' words keep something of the original French pronunciation, but the accent marks are sometimes omitted.

The following is a list of some of the most important Gallicisms. Note that we often have no exact equivalents: hence the use of the French phrases.

Try to discover some more Gallicisms (and their meaning in English) to add to the list.

à la carte - a meal ordered course by course as you wish.
au pair - a girl from abroad helping with housework in return for room and board.
au revoir - goodbye, until we meet again.
avant-garde - innovators in any art in a particular period.
bistro - a small bar, or restaurant.
boutique - a small shop selling clothes.
carte blanche - the freedom to do exactly as you like.
chic - stylishness; elegance in dress.
coup d'état - a violent or illegal change in government.
cuisine - a style of cooking.
cul-de-sac - a street or passage closed at one end.
début - a performer's first appearance.
déjà vu - illusory feeling of having already experienced a present situation.
dénouement - the unravelling of the plot in a play or film.
discothèque - a club ('disco') where records or tapes are played for dancing.
encore - a call by an appreciative audience for a further item.
en route - on the way; while travelling.
fait accompli - a thing already done and therefore not worth arguing against.
faux pas - an indiscreet offence by speech or action against social convention.
Grand Prix - motor-racing championship event in any country, held under international rules.
hors d'oeuvre - a light course served to begin a main meal.
née - used to show a woman's maiden name.
pièce de résistance - the most important or remarkable item; the most important dish at a special meal.
précis - a short summing-up; a summary.
rendezvous - a meeting-place previously agreed upon.
table d'hôte - a meal which is served at a stated fixed price.
tête-à-tête - a conversation between two persons only.